COPYRIGHT

CONTRIBUTORS

CURTIS G. BENJAMIN
McGraw-Hill Publishing Co., New York, New York

MICHAEL A. DUGGAN
Professor, Department of General Business
University of Texas, Austin, Texas

ABE A. GOLDMAN
General Counsel, Office of Copyright
Library of Congress, Washington, D.C.

CHARLES F. GOSNELL, M.S., Ph.D.
Director of Libraries
Professor of Library Administration
New York University Libraries, Washington Square, New York, New York

J. CLEMENT HARRISON, D.P.A., M.S., F.L.A.
Director, School of Library Science
University of Dalhousie, Halifax, Canada

ALLEN KENT
Director, Office of Communications Programs, and Professor
University of Pittsburgh

JOSEPH H. KUNEY
Director of Business Operations and Publications Research
American Chemical Society, Washington, D.C.

DAN LACY
Senior Vice President, McGraw-Hill Publishing Co., New York, New York

WILLIAM Z. NASRI, B.A., LL.B., M.L.S.
Research Associate, Graduate School of Library and
Information Sciences and the Knowledge Availability Systems Center
University of Pittsburgh

LYMAN RAY PATTERSON
Professor of Law
Vanderbilt University, Nashville, Tennessee

COPYRIGHT
Current Viewpoints on History, Laws, Legislation

EDITED BY ALLEN KENT AND HAROLD LANCOUR

Graduate School of Library and Information Sciences
and The Knowledge Availability Systems Center
University of Pittsburgh
Pittsburgh, Pennsylvania

R.R. BOWKER COMPANY,   New York & London,   1972

Published by R. R. Bowker Co. (a Xerox company)
1180 Avenue of the Americas
New York, N.Y. 10036

Originally published in the
Encyclopedia of Library and Information Science,
Volume 6, published by Marcel Dekker, Inc.
Executive Editors, Allen Kent and Harold Lancour
Assistant Editor, William Z. Nasri.

International Standard Book Number: 0-8352-0542-8
Library of Congress Catalog Card Number: 72-774
Printed and bound in the United States of America
Reprinted with the permission of Marcel Dekker, Inc.

CONTENTS

PREFACE

Man's struggle to maintain freedom of action has traditionally been confounded by the need of society to impose controls. This need finds its rationale in attempting to assure that individual freedom does not impinge too much on the rights of others.

The freedom to read is now accepted as the right of any individual, and attempts to limit this right often lead to legal tests. But how far this right extends is a question that has become increasingly important and interesting as technology has made it possible and even cost effective to copy published materials, to record the materials in computer-processable form, and to transmit images of the published materials over considerable distances.

When an individual purchases a book, he presumably owns the book. What are the rights of ownership? To destroy the book—certainly! To loan the book—probably, at least precedent in libraries suggests this right. But to copy or transmit parts or all of the material is the sticking point insofar as rights are concerned—because here impingement on the rights of the publisher may eventually be at risk.

The issue has so many facets, and the need to resolve it is so timely, that the viewpoints of the potential protagonists need to be aired, especially as new copyright legislation is being studied and debated.

Originally prepared for publication in the *Encyclopedia of Library and Information Science,* the material that follows seemed worthy of wide dissemination as a separate book. It is hoped that *Copyright: Current Viewpoints on History, Laws, Legislation,* published by R. R. Bowker, will be a welcome addition to the shelves of large public libraries, academic libraries, law libraries, and publishing firms.

ALLEN KENT

March 15, 1972

Introduction

The exclusive, legally secured, right to publish and sell the substance and form of a literary, musical, or artistic work is what is meant by copyright.

Means of *publishing* and *forms* of works are legion. If the *form* is a printed page, modern technology permits images to be transmitted over distances and brought to the simultaneous attention of many persons.

Indiscriminate access to these images may prevent the copyright holder from recovering the cost of publication, and thus remove the incentive to distribute the work—the very incentive that copyright is to encourage. On the other hand, restricting access may inhibit the incentive to use the work, which is contrary to the interests of the author and the public, and to the intent of the copyright legislation.

The copyright legislation in force in the United States today is based on a society that existed in 1909. The technology relating to printing, copying, communicating, and computing has changed dramatically during the six decades since the basic legislation passed. Few of those who are involved with, or are influenced by, copyright feel that their interests are fairly represented. But none have been able to propose new legislation which would represent a reasonable consensus of diverging opinion with regard to how the law should be changed.

It should be no surprise, therefore, that there are many advocacy positions taken in discussion of copyright. It did not seem possible to represent, in one definitive article, the various points of view. Rather, an attempt has been made in the following to lay out as many of the factors involved as could be identified—in separate signed articles.

There is no *one* sequence that could be followed so that the advocates of each point of view might feel that their case was presented in proper context. However, some sequence was needed—the following being the best compromise that the editors could arrange.

History

Copyright, as it is understood today, i.e., the right generally secured by law to authors of literary, dramatic, musical, and artistic works to authorize the production or reproduction of such works, has its statutory beginnings in the British Copyright Act of 1709 (by modern reckoning 1710) or the Statute of Anne. This "Act for the Encouragement of Learning by Vesting the Copies of Printed Books in the Authors or Purchasers of Such Copies During the Times Therein Mentioned" gave legal recognition to the position of the author for the first time in history. The act has further significance in that it was a successor to a series of privileges, monopolies, decrees, and licensing acts in sixteenth- and seventeenth-century England that had been designed to maintain governmental control of the press and the monopolistic position of the Stationers' Company (incorporated by the Crown in 1557) rather

1

than the rights of the author. If it can be said that "copyright" existed before 1709, it might best be defined as "stationer's copyright" or "publisher's copyright" and not copyright as understood by the British Parliament when it placed the Act of Anne on the statute book. The Statute of Anne is also of special significance in the history of copyright in the United States. It was to serve as a model for the early copyright acts of the states and for the first federal act passed in 1790.

The Act of 1709 decreed that the authors of all works not yet published were to be granted the sole rights for a period of 14 years. At the end of this 14 years the copyright was to remain with the author, if living, for an additional 14 years. It seems clear from this that the intention was to put an end to what had been popularly conceived as "permanent copyright" during the preceding 150 years, with this "right" belonging to the stationer who had made a prepublication entry in the Registers of the Stationers' Company in London. Despite this provision in the Statute of Anne, it was not until 1774, when the House of Lords gave its decision on the duration of copyright in the *Donaldson* v. *Beckett* case, that it was clearly established that no permanent copyright could be held to exist. Later, in 1834, the United States Supreme Court came to the same decision in the *Wheaton* case.

The Statute of Anne added six deposit libraries (five of them in Scotland) to the three already enjoying this privilege under the licensing acts of the previous century. Provision for legal deposit was to be made in almost all subsequent British copyright acts, but recent legislation has made it clear that copyright under British law is in no way dependent upon deposit in the six libraries in the British Isles now designated as legal deposit libraries, viz., the British Museum, the Bodleian Library, Cambridge University Library, the National Library of Scotland, the National Library of Wales, and Trinity College, Dublin. Failure to deposit, according to the appropriate statutory provisions, is a punishable offence on the part of the publisher; it in no way deprives the copyright owner of his right.

The British Copyright Act of 1911 abolished the necessity for registration of copyright, in compliance with Article 4 of the Berne Convention. Copyright under British law now comes into existence automatically on publication of the work, and its duration is the lifetime of the author and a period of 50 years after his death.

The first copyright provisions in the United States followed the British statutes very closely. Between 1783 and 1786 every state except Delaware passed copyright legislation along similar lines.

The first United States Copyright Act was passed in 1790. The period of copyright, following British precedent, was 14 years, with renewal possible for an additional 14 years. Among the detailed provisions made in this act were deposit of the title page of the book before publication, and deposit of a copy of the book itself with the United States Secretary of State within 6 months of publication. The Act of 1802 provided for the printing of copyright information in every book. In 1831 the period of copyright was extended to 28 years, with a period of renewal of 14 years. In 1846 two deposit copies were asked for, one for the Library of Congress (established in 1800) and one for the Smithsonian Institution (established in 1846). In 1870 the Copyright Office was established within the Library of Congress, which became the sole recipient of deposited works. Two copies were to be deposited. In 1874 details of the notice to appear in all copyrighted publications were specified as the word "Copyright," the date, and the name of the copyright owner.

The Chace Act, passed in 1891, extended copyright protection to foreign authors, but at the same time introduced the "manufacturing clause," insisting upon the manufacture of their publications in the United States and the inclusion of a notice of United States copyright.

Today, under the Copyright Act of 1909, the period of United States copyright is 28 years from the date of publication. The renewal period is also 28 years.

Recent efforts to revise the United States Copyright Act have included provisions to extend the second 28 year period of existing copyrights to 47 years, making a maximum period of 75 years. Copyrights on new works would last for the author's lifetime and 50 years after his death. This latter provision, if enacted, would bring the United States into line with many other countries, notably in Europe, in accordance with the recommendation on the subject of UNESCO in its Universal Copyright Convention (1952), to which the United States is a signatory.

Serious and prolonged attempts to carry through a major revision of United States copyright law have been made in every recent Congress and an impressive collection of Congressional Hearings and other publications on the subject can now be found on the shelves of the country's libraries, information centers, and publishing houses. Contributions by representatives of these various conflicting interests, including the authors, follow this brief historical introduction. A reading of them will afford some explanation of Congress's delay and difficulties. Before and since Queen Anne's Statute the rights of those who write and publish and the interests of those who use what is written and published have come into conflict. It has been a state of "continuing discontent," in the words of Lyman Ray Patterson. How different things might have been had Samuel Johnson been in error when he told us 200 years ago that "No man but a blockhead ever wrote except for money!"

SELECTED BIBLIOGRAPHY

Binns, Norman E., *An Introduction to Historical Bibliography,* 2nd ed., Association of Assistant Librarians, London, 1962.

Mumby, Frank Arthur, *Publishing and Bookselling: A History from the Earliest Times to the Present Day,* 4th ed., Cape, London, 1956.

Partridge, R. D. B., *A History of the Legal Deposit of Books Throughout the British Empire,* Library Association, London, 1938.

Patterson, Lyman Ray, *Copyright in Historical Perspective,* Vanderbilt Univ. Press, Nashville, Tennessee, 1968.

Pilpel, Harriet F., and Morton David Goldberg, *A Copyright Guide,* Bowker, New York, 1969.

Plant, M., *English Book Trade,* Allen & Unwin, London, 1939.

J. CLEMENT HARRISON

The Factual—U.S. Copyright

I. THE CONSTITUTIONAL PROVISION RESPECTING COPYRIGHT

The Congress shall have Power . . . To promote the Progress of Science and useful Arts, by securing for limited Times to Authors and Inventors the exclusive Right to their respective Writing and Discoveries. (U. S. Const. Art. I, § 8)

II. COPYRIGHT LAW OF U.S. ; U.S. CODE, TITLE 17*

§ 1. EXCLUSIVE RIGHTS AS TO COPYRIGHTED WORKS.—Any person entitled thereto, upon complying with the provisions of this title, shall have the exclusive right:

(a) To print, reprint, publish, copy, and vend the copyrighted work;

(b) To translate the copyrighted work into other languages or dialects, or make any other version thereof, if it be a literary work; to dramatize it if it be a nondramatic work; to convert it into a novel or other nondramatic work if it be a drama; to arrange or adapt it if it be a musical work; to complete, execute, and finish it if it be a model or design for a work of art;

(c) To deliver, authorize the delivery of, read, or present the copyrighted work in public for profit if it be a lecture, sermon, address or similar production, or other nondramatic literary work; to make or procure the making of any transcription or record thereof by or from which, in whole or in part, it may in any manner or by any method be exhibited, delivered, presented, produced, or reproduced; and to play or perform it in public for profit, and to exhibit, represent, produce, or reproduce it in any manner or by any method whatsoever. The damages for the infringement by broadcast of any work referred to in this subsection shall not exceed the sum of $100 where the infringing broadcaster shows that he was not aware that he was infringing and that such infringement could not have been reasonably foreseen; and

(d) To perform or represent the copyrighted work publicly if it be a drama or, if it be a dramatic work and not reproduced in copies for sale, to vend any manuscript or any record whatsoever thereof; to make or to procure the making of any transcription or record thereof by or from which, in whole or in part, it may in any manner or by any method be exhibited, performed, represented, produced, or reproduced; and to exhibit, perform, represent, produce, or reproduce it in any manner or by any method whatsoever; and

(e) To perform the copyrighted work publicly for profit if it be a musical composition; and for the purpose of public performance for profit, and for the purposes set forth in subsection (a) hereof, to make any arrangements or setting of it or of the melody of it in any system of notation or any form of record in which the thought of an author may be recorded and from which it may be read or reproduced.

§ 2. RIGHTS OF AUTHOR OR PROPRIETOR OF UNPUBLISHED WORK.—Nothing in this title shall be construed to annul or limit the right of the author or proprietor of an unpublished work, at common law or in equity, to prevent the copying, publication, or use of such unpublished work without his consent, and to obtain damages therefor.

§ 3. PROTECTION OF COMPONENT PARTS OF WORK COPYRIGHTED; COMPOSITE WORKS OR PERIODICALS.—The copyright provided by this title shall protect all the copyrightable component parts of the work copyrighted, and all matter therein in which copyright is already subsisting, but without extending the duration or scope of such copyright. The copyright upon composite works or periodicals shall give to the proprietor thereof all the rights in respect thereto which he would have if each part were individually copyrighted under this title.

*Only relevant sections are given here.

§ 4. ALL WRITINGS OF AUTHOR INCLUDED.—The works for which copyright may be secured under this title shall include all the writings of an author.

§ 5. CLASSIFICATION OF WORKS FOR REGISTRATION.—The application for registration shall specify to which of the following classes the work in which copyright is claimed belongs:

(a) Books, including composite and cyclopedic works, directories, gazetteers, and other compilations.

(b) Periodicals, including newspapers.

(c) Lectures, sermons, addresses (prepared for oral delivery).

(d) Dramatic or dramatico-musical compositions.

(e) Musical compositions.

(f) Maps.

(g) Works of art; models or designs for works of art.

(h) Reproductions of a work of art.

(i) Drawings or plastic works of a scientific or technical character.

(j) Photographs.

(k) Prints and pictorial illustrations including prints or labels used for articles of merchandise.

(l) Motion-picture photoplays.

(m) Motion pictures other than photoplays.

§ 7. COPYRIGHT ON COMPILATIONS OF WORKS IN PUBLIC DOMAIN OR OF COPYRIGHTED WORKS; SUBSISTING COPYRIGHTS NOT AFFECTED.—Compilations or abridgements, adaptation, arrangements, dramatizations, translations, or other versions of works in the public domain or of copyrighted works when produced with the consent of the proprietor of the copyright in such works, or works republished with new matter, shall be regarded as new works subject to copyright under the provisions of this title; but the publication of any such new works shall not affect the force or validity of any subsisting copyright upon the matter employed or any part thereof, or be construed to imply an exclusive right to such use of the original works, or to secure or extend copyright in such original works.

§ 8. COPYRIGHT NOT TO SUBSIST IN WORKS IN PUBLIC DOMAIN, OR PUBLISHED PRIOR TO JULY 1, 1909, AND NOT ALREADY COPYRIGHTED, OR GOVERNMENT PUBLICATIONS; PUBLICATION BY GOVERNMENT OF COPYRIGHTED MATERIAL.—No copyright shall subsist in the original text of any work which is in the public domain, or in any work which was published in this country or any foreign country prior to July 1, 1909, and has not been already copyrighted in the United States, or in any publication of the United States Government, or any reprint, in whole or in part, thereof, except that the Postmaster General may secure copyright on behalf of the United States in the whole or any part of the publications authorized by section 2506 of title 39.

The publication or republication by the Government, either separately or in a public document, of any material in which copyright is subsisting shall not be taken to cause any abridgement or annulment of the copyright or to authorize any use or appropriation of such copyright material without the consent of the copyright proprietor.

§10. PUBLICATION OF WORK WITH NOTICE.—Any person entitled thereto by this title may secure copyright for his work by publication thereof with the notice of copyright required by this title; and such notice shall be affixed to each copy thereof published or offered for sale in the United States by authority of the copyright proprietor, except in the case of books seeking ad interim protection under section 22 of this title.

§ 13. DEPOSIT OF COPIES AFTER PUBLICATION; ACTION OR PROCEEDING FOR INFRINGEMENT.—After copyright has been secured by publication of the work with the notice of copyright as provided in section 10 of this title, there shall be promptly deposited in the Copyright Office or in the mail addressed to the Register of Copyrights, Washington, District of Columbia, two complete copies of the best edition thereof then published . . .

§ 24. DURATION; RENEWAL AND EXTENSION.—The copyright secured by this title shall endure for twenty-eight years from the date of first publication, whether the copyrighted work bears the author's true name or is published anonymously or under an assumed name: *Provided,* That in the case of any posthumous work or of any periodical, cyclopedic, or other composite work upon which the copyright was originally secured by the proprietor thereof, or of any work copyrighted by a corporate body (otherwise than as assignee or licensee of the individual author) or by an employer for whom such work is made for hire, the proprietor of such copyright shall be entitled to a renewal and extension of the copyright in such work for the further term of twenty-eight years when application for such renewal and extension shall have been made to the copyright office and duly registered therein within one year prior to the expiration of the original term of copyright: *And provided further,* That in the case of any other copyrighted work, including a contribution by an individual author to a periodical or to a cyclopedic or other composite work, the author of such work, if still living, or the widow, widower, or children of the author, if the author be not living, or if such author, widow, widower, or children be not living, then the author's executors, or in the absence of a will, his next of kin shall be entitled to a renewal and extension of the copyright in such work for a further term of twenty-eight years when application for such renewal and extension shall have been made to the copyright office and duly registered therein within one year prior to the expiration of the original term of copyright: *And provided further,* That in default of the registration of such application for renewal and extension, the copyright in any work shall determine at the expiration of twenty-eight years from first publication.

§ 25. RENEWAL OF COPYRIGHTS REGISTERED IN PATENT OFFICE UNDER REPEALED LAW.— Subsisting copyrights originally registered in the Patent Office prior to July 1, 1940, under section 3 of the act of June 18, 1874, shall be subject to renewal in behalf of the proprietor upon application made to the Register of Copyrights within one year prior to the expiration of the original term of twenty-eight years.

§ 26. TERMS DEFINED.—In the interpretation and construction of this title "the date of publication" shall in the case of a work of which copies are reproduced for sale or distribution be held to be the earliest date when copies of the first authorized edition were placed on sale, sold, or publicly distributed by the proprietor of the copyright or under his authority, and the word "author" shall include an employer in the case of works made for hire.

§ 101. INFRINGEMENT.—If any person shall infringe the copyright in any work protected under the copyright laws of the United States such person shall be liable:

(a) INJUNCTION.—To an injunction restraining such infringement;

(b) DAMAGES AND PROFITS; AMOUNT; OTHER REMEDIES.—To pay to the copyright proprietor such damages as the copyright proprietor may have suffered due to the infringement, as well as all the profits which the infringer shall have made from such infringement, and in proving profits the plaintiff shall be required to prove sales only, and the defendant shall be required to prove every element of cost which he claims, or in lieu of actual damages and profits, such damages as to the court shall appear to be just . . .

III. AMENDMENTS

Title 17 of the U.S. Code, which is the current law on copyright, is based on the Act of March 4, 1909. Title 17, however, passed through several amendments since its codification and enactment on July 30, 1947. It was first amended by an act on April 27, 1948, changing the price of the catalog of the titles of the articles deposited and registered for copyright from $10 to $25. The amendment also raised the general fee for registration from $2 to $6 for a print or label used for articles of merchandise, and to $4 for any other work.

The second amendment was on June 25, 1948, and it repealed some sections relating to the judicial proceedings.

The next amendment was on June 3, 1949, wherein copyright protection was extended to periodicals of foreign origin to match the protection previously granted to books of foreign origin. It also raised the period for deposit of one complete copy of the foreign materials in the copyright office from within 60 days to 6 months after its publication abroad. In addition, the amendment extended the ad interim protection from 4 months from date of deposit to 5 years from the date of publication abroad. It also permitted the deposit of copies and catalog cards for foreign works in lieu of payment of the copyright fees ($4).

It was necessary, on October 31, 1951, to pass an amendatory act correcting a number of technical discrepancies (e.g., spelling) in the copyright law.

Later, the Congress passed an amendatory act on July 17, 1952, extending the protection to public performance and recording rights for nondramatic literary works.

Another amendment was passed on April 13, 1954, indicating that if the last day for taking an action (e.g., deposit of a work) falls on Saturday or Sunday or a holiday, such action may be taken on the next succeeding business day.

On August 31, 1954, the Congress approved an amendment relating to the coming into force in the U.S. of the Universal Convention and the relaxation of the manufactory clause regarding works of foreign origin.

Two years later, on March 29, 1956, an amendatory act was passed permitting the deposit of photographs or other identifying reproductions in lieu of published or reproduction of work of art, drawings, or plastic works of scientific or technical character, prints, illustrations, and labels used for articles of merchandise.

On September 7, 1957, another amendment prohibited criminal or civil proceedings under the provision of Title 17, unless it is commenced within 3 years after the cause of action arose or the claim occurred.

On September 7, 1962, the copyright law was amended again to improve the language of the code, and on September 19, another amendatory act extended the duration of copyright protection subsisting in any work prior to December 31, 1965, to continue until December 31, 1965. This was repeated in each consecutive year.

On December 16, 1969, an amendatory act extended the duration of copyright protection for works expiring before December 31, 1970, to continue until this date. This same amendment was repeated in 1970. The reason was the revision of the copyright law which is still under consideration by the U.S. Senate.

WILLIAM Z. NASRI

The Factual—International Copyright

The clause of the U.S. Constitution on which the copyright law is established "... to promote the progress of Science and useful Arts ..." is a concept underlying all contemporary copyright laws. The details of each law, however, vary among countries and the scope of rights granted to the author vary accordingly. In addition, each national law is concerned about its authors and usually discriminates against foreigners. A contradiction also exists between the protection of national property and the fact that literary and artistic works are increasingly the object of worldwide exploitation (reproduction, translation, broadcasting, transmission, etc.). Thus, the authors in each country, concerned about the protection of their works in another country, would have no other recourse but the national laws of the latter. Therefore, it appeared that the establishment of uniform copyright protection all over the world was necessary in order to create a common legal base according to which the exploitation of works and the payment of rights could be effected.

In 1863 a small group of countries' representatives convened in Berne (Switzerland) and signed the Berne Convention to forbid all discrimination against foreign authors and to establish a uniform treatment (Unionist treatment) regarding the protection of copyrighted works. Presently, the Berne Convention is in effect between sixty countries. The United States, however, is not among them (see Appendix 1). This convention has been revised by successive conferences, the last of which was at Stockholm in July 1967. The revision was mainly to improve the existing rules and to add a Protocol providing additional exceptions in order to help developing countries (e.g., royalties for translation).

The agreement determines for each country the territory to which the convention applies and the effective date depends on the convention itself according to the ratification or consent of any given country. It applies only to works that have not fallen into the public domain in their country of origin or in the country where the protection is claimed.

The Berne Convention terms regarding the length of protection are important because the duration is unequal in different countries and the authors naturally want to impose the longest possible period. Accordingly, the duration of protection, in principle, is for the life of the author and for an additional 50 years after his death (for more details see Appendix 2).

The Berne Convention was administered by the United International Bureaux for the Protection of Intellectual Property (BIRPI). Later, because of its worldwide application the bureaux had to become an organization attached to the United Nations. The convention also gives the power to the International Court of Justice for the settlement of all differences concerning its interpretation or application.

After World War II, the foreign market for the United States copyrighted material was expanded. It was also clear that the U.S. would not join the Berne Convention, as it "has found it impossible to subscribe to the [Berne] Convention . . . because it embodied concepts at variance with American Copyright Law. These concepts involved such matters as the automatic recognition of copyright without any formalities, the protection of "moral" rights and the retroactivity of copyright protection with respect to works which are already in the public domain in the United States. This revival of copyright under the retroactivity doctrine would have worked considerable prejudice to American motion picture, music, and publishing houses. . . . Finally it was claimed that Berne's protection of "oral" works, such as speeches, would have conflicted with Article I, Section 8 of the Constitution, which refers only to "writings" as material to be protected" (1).

Accordingly, new efforts were directed at preparing an international convention to which the member countries and the nonmembers of the Berne Convention might adhere and by September 1952 forty countries, including the United States, convened in Geneva and signed the Universal Copyright Convention which was and still is open to adherence by other countries as well (2). The Geneva Convention "embodies the most acceptable concepts of American and European practice . . . [and] recognizes the basic principles governing the Law of Copyright in the United States."(3) It leaves great freedom to the joining country to protect or not protect according to its national laws, thus providing the authors with more limited protection than did the Berne Convention. Presently, fifty-five countries have signed (see Appendix 3). Similar to the Berne Convention, the Universal Copyright Convention does not apply to works that have fallen into the public domain in any country at the effective date of the convention in that country. The duration of protection is that of the country where protection is claimed. However, the latter has the right to limit the protection to the duration accorded in the country of origin.

Finally, it is interesting to note that the Berne Convention provides protection for authors, while Universal Copyright Convention protects works. (For more details see Appendix 4).

APPENDIX 1

BERNE UNION MEMBER COUNTRIES*

As of July 1, 1970

Argentina	Greece	New Zealand
Australia	Holy See	Niger
Austria	Hungary	Norway
Belgium	Iceland	Pakistan
Brazil	India	Philippines
Bulgaria	Ireland	Poland
Cameroon	Israel	Portugal
Canada	Italy	Rumania
Ceylon	Ivory Coast	Senegal
Chile	Japan	South Africa
Congo (Brazzaville)	Lebanon	Spain
Congo (Kinshasa)	Liechtenstein	Sweden
Cyprus	Luxembourg	Switzerland
Czechoslovakia	Madagascar	Thailand
Dahomey	Mali	Tunisia
Denmark	Malta	Turkey
Finland	Mexico	United Kingdom
France	Monaco	Upper Volta
Gabon	Morocco	Uruguay
Germany (Fed. Rep.)	Netherlands	Yugoslavia

*"State of the International Union on July 1, 1970," *Copyright (BIRPI),* **6** (7), 120–121 (July 1970).

APPENDIX 2

INTERNATIONAL CONVENTION REVISING THE BERNE CONVENTION FOR THE PROTECTION OF LITERARY AND ARTISTIC WORKS, SIGNED ON 9 SEPTEMBER, 1886; COMPLETED AT PARIS, 4 MAY, 1896; REVISED AT BERLIN, 13 NOVEMBER, 1908; COMPLETED AT BERNE, 20 MARCH, 1914 AND REVISED AT ROME, 2 JUNE, 1928

Brussels 26th June 1948

Australia, Austria, Belgium, Brazil, Canada, Czechoslovakia, Denmark, Finland, France, Greece, Hungary, Iceland, India, Ireland, Italy, Lebanon, Liechtenstein, Luxembourg, Monaco, Morocco, New Zealand, the Netherlands, Norway, Pakistan, Poland, Portugal, Spain, Sweden, Switzerland, Syria, Tunis, the Union of South Africa, the United Kingdom of Great Britain and Northern Ireland, Vatican City and Yugoslavia.

Being equally animated by the desire to protect in as effective and uniform a manner as possible the rights of authors over their literary and artistic works,

Have resolved to revise and to complete the Act signed at Berne on the 9th September 1886,[1] completed at Paris on the 4th May 1896,[2] revised at Berlin on the 13th November 1908,[3] completed at Berne on the 20th March 1914[4] and revised at Rome on the 2nd June 1928.[5]

Consequently, the undersigned Plenipotentiaries, having presented their full powers, recognised as in good and due form, have agreed as follows:

ARTICLE 1

The countries to which this Convention applies constitute a Union for the protection of the rights of authors over their literary and artistic works.

ARTICLE 2

(1) The term "literary and artistic works" shall include every production in the literary, scientific and artistic domain, whatever may be the mode or form of its expression, such as books, pamphlets and other writings; lectures, addresses, sermons and other works of the same nature; dramatic or dramatico-musical works, choreographic works and entertainments in dumb show, the acting form of which is fixed in writing or otherwise; musical compositions with or without words; cinematographic works and works produced by a process analogous to cinematography; works of drawing, painting, architecture, sculpture, engraving and lithography; photographic works and works produced by a process analogous to photography; works of applied art, illustrations, geographical charts, plans, sketches and plastic works relative to geography, topography, architecture or science.

(2) Translations, adaptations, arrangements of music and other alterations of a literary or artistic work shall be protected as original works without prejudice to the rights of the author of the original work. It shall, however, be a matter for legislation in the countries of the Union to determine the protection to be granted to translations of official texts of a legislative, administrative and legal nature.

[1] "Switzerland No. 1 (1887)," C. 5167.
[2] "Treaty Series No. 14 (1897)," C. 8681.
[3] "Treaty Series No. 19 (1912)," Cd. 6324.
[4] "Treaty Series No. 11 (1914)," Cd. 7613.
[5] "Treaty Series No. 12 (1932)," Cmd. 4057.

(3) Collections of literary or artistic works such as encyclopedias and anthologies which by reason of the selection and arrangements of their contents constitute intellectual creations shall be protected as such without prejudice to the rights of the authors in respect of each of the works forming part of such collections.

(4) The works mentioned in this Article shall enjoy protection in all countries of the Union. This protection shall operate for the benefit of the author and his legal representatives and assignees.

(5) It shall be a matter for legislation in the countries of the Union to determine the extent of the application of their laws to works of applied art and industrial designs and models, as well as the conditions under which such works, designs and models shall be protected. Works protected in the country of origin solely as designs and models shall be entitled in other countries of the Union only to such protection as shall be accorded to designs and models in such countries.

ARTICLE 2*bis*

(1) It shall be a matter for legislation in the countries of the Union to exclude wholly or in part from the protection afforded by the preceding Article political speeches and speeches delivered in the course of legal proceedings.

(2) It shall also be a matter for legislation in the countries of the Union to determine the conditions under which lectures, addresses, sermons and other works of the same nature may be reproduced by the press.

(3) Nevertheless, the author alone shall have the right of making a collection of his works mentioned in the above paragraphs.

ARTICLE 3
(omitted)

ARTICLE 4

(1) Authors who are nationals of any of the countries of the Union shall enjoy in countries other than the country of origin of the work, for their works, whether unpublished or first published in a country of the Union, the rights which their respective laws do now or may hereafter grant to their nationals, as well as the rights specially granted by this Convention.

(2) The enjoyment and the exercise of these rights shall not be subject to any formality; such enjoyment and such exercise shall be independent of the existence of protection in the country of origin of the work. Consequently, apart from the provisions of this Convention, the extent of protection, as well as the means of redress afforded to the author to protect his right, shall be governed exclusively by the laws of the country where protection is claimed.

(3) The country of origin shall be considered to be, in the case of published works, the country of first publication, even in the case of works published simultaneously in several countries of the Union which grant the same term of protection; in the case of works published simultaneously in several countries of the Union which grant different terms of protection, the country of which the legislation grants the shortest term of protection. In the case of works published simultaneously in a country outside the Union and in a country of the Union, the latter country shall be considered exclusively as the country of origin. A work shall be considered as having been published simultaneously in several countries which has been published in two or more countries within thirty days of its first publication.

(4) For the purposes of Articles 4, 5 and 6, "published works" shall be understood to be works copies of which have been issued and made available in sufficient quantities to the public, whatever may be the means of manufacture of the copies. The presentation of a dra-

matic, dramatico-musical or cinematographic work, the performance of a musical work, the public recitation of a literary work, the transmission or the radio-diffusion of literary or artistic works, the exhibition of a work of art and the construction of a work of architecture shall not constitute publication.

(5) The country of origin shall be considered to be, in the case of unpublished works, the country to which the author belongs. However, in the case of works of architecture, or of graphic and plastic works forming part of a building, the country of the Union where these works have been built or incorporated in a building shall be considered as the country of origin.

ARTICLE 5

Authors who are nationals of one of the countries of the Union, and who first publish their works in another country of the Union, shall have in the latter country the same rights as native authors.

ARTICLE 6

(1) Authors who are not nationals of one of the countries of the Union, and who first publish their works in one of those countries, shall enjoy in that country the same rights as native authors, and in the other countries of the Union the rights granted by this Convention.

(2) Nevertheless, where any country outside the Union fails to protect in an adequate manner the works of authors who are nationals of one of the countries of the Union, the latter country may restrict the protection given to the works of authors who are, at the date of the first publication thereof, nationals of the other country and are not effectively domiciled in one of the countries of the Union. If the country of first publication avails itself of this right, the other countries of the Union shall not be required to grant to works thus subjected to special treatment a wider protection than that granted to them in the country of first publication.

(3) No restrictions introduced by virtue of the preceding paragraph shall affect the rights which an author may have acquired in respect of a work published in a country of the Union before such restrictions were put into force.

(4) The countries of the Union which restrict the grant of copyright in accordance with this Article shall give notice thereof to the Government of the Swiss Confederation by a written declaration specifying the countries in regard to which protection is restricted, and the restrictions to which rights of authors who are nationals of those countries are subjected. The Government of the Swiss Confederation shall immediately communicate this declaration to all the countries of the Union.

ARTICLE 6*bis*

(1) Independently of the author's copyright, and even after the transfer of the said copyright, the author shall have the right, during his lifetime, to claim authorship of the work and to object to any distortion, mutilation or other alteration thereof, or any other action in relation to the said work which would be prejudicial to his honour or reputation.

(2) In so far as the legislation of the countries of the Union permits, the rights granted to the author in accordance with the preceding paragraph shall, after his death, be maintained, at least until the expiry of the copyright, and shall be exercisable by the persons or institutions authorised by said legislation. The determination of the conditions under which the rights mentioned in this paragraph shall be exercised shall be governed by the legislation of the countries of the Union.

(3) The means of redress for safeguarding the rights granted by this Article shall be governed by the legislation of the country where protection is claimed.

ARTICLE 7

(1) The term of protection granted by this Convention shall be the life of the author and fifty years after his death.

(2) However, where one or more countries of the Union grant a term of protection in excess of that provided by paragraph (1), the term shall be governed by the law of the country where protection is claimed, but shall not exceed the term fixed in the country of origin of the work.

(3) In the case of cinematographic and photographic works, as well as works produced by a process analogous to cinematography or photography, and in the case of works of applied art, the term of protection shall be governed by the law of the country where protection is claimed, but shall not exceed the term fixed in the country of origin of the work.

(4) In the case of anonymous and pseudonymous works the term of protection shall be fixed at fifty years from the date of their publication. However, when the pseudonym adopted by the author leaves no doubt as to his identity, the term of protection shall be that provided in paragraph (1). If the author of an anonymous or pseudonymous work discloses his identity during the above-mentioned period, the term of protection applicable shall be that provided in paragraph (1).

(5) In the case of posthumous works which do not fall within the categories of works included in paragraphs (3) and (4) the term of the protection afforded to the heirs and the legal representatives and assignees of the author shall end at the expiry of fifty years after the death of the author.

(6) The term of protection subsequent to the death of the author and the terms provided by paragraphs (3), (4) and (5) shall run from the date of his death or of publication, but such terms shall always be deemed to begin on the 1st January of the year following the event which gives rise to them.

ARTICLE 7bis

In the case of a work of joint authorship the term of protection shall be calculated from the date of the death of the last surviving author.

ARTICLE 8

Authors of literary and artistic works protected by this Convention shall have the exclusive right of making and of authorising the translation of their works throughout the term of protection of their rights in the original works.

ARTICLE 9

(1) Serial novels, short stories and all other works, whether literary, scientific or artistic, whatever their purpose, and which are published in the newspapers or periodicals of one of the countries of the Union shall not be reproduced in the other countries without the consent of the authors.

(2) Articles on current economic, political or religious topics may be reproduced by the press unless the reproduction thereof is expressly reserved; nevertheless, the source must always be clearly indicated. The legal consequences of the breach of this obligation shall be determined by the laws of the country where protection is claimed.

(3) The protection of this Convention shall not apply to news of the day nor to miscellaneous information having the character of mere items of news.

ARTICLE 10

(1) It shall be permissible in all the countries of the Union to make short quotations from newspaper articles and periodicals, as well as to include them in press summaries.

(2) The right to include excerpts from literary or artistic works in educational or scientific publications, or in chrestomathies, in so far as this inclusion is justified by its purpose, shall be a matter for legislation in the countries of the Union, and for special arrangements existing or to be concluded between them.

(3) Quotations and excerpts shall be accompanied by an acknowledgment of the source and by the name of the author, if his name appears thereon.

ARTICLE 10*bis*

It shall be a matter for legislation in countries of the Union to determine the conditions under which recording, reproduction, and public communication of short extracts from literary and artistic works may be made for the purpose of reporting current events by means of photography or cinematography or by radio-diffusion.

ARTICLE 11

(1) The authors of dramatic, dramatico-musical or musical works shall enjoy the exclusive right of authorising: i. the public presentation and public performance of their works; ii. the public distribution by any means of the presentation and performance of their works. The application of the provisions of Articles 11*bis* and 13 is, however, reserved.

(2) Authors of dramatic or dramatico-musical works, during the full term of their rights over the original works, shall enjoy the same rights with respect to translations thereof.

(3) In order to enjoy the protection of this Article, authors shall not be bound, when publishing their works, to forbid the public presentation or performance thereof.

ARTICLE 11*bis*

(1) Authors of literary and artistic works shall have the exclusive right of authorising: i. the radio-diffusion of their works or the communication thereof to the public by any other means of wireless diffusion of signs, sounds or images; ii. any communication to the public whether over wires or not, of the radio-diffusion of the work, when this communication is made by a body other than the original one; iii. the communication to the public by loudspeaker or any other similar instrument transmitting, by signs, sounds or images, the radio-diffusion of the work.

(2) It shall be a matter for legislation in the countries of the Union to determine the conditions under which the rights mentioned in the preceding paragraph may be exercised, but these conditions shall apply only in the countries where they have been prescribed. They shall not in any circumstances be prejudicial to the moral right of the author, nor to his right to obtain just remuneration which, in the absence of agreement, shall be fixed by competent authority.

(3) Except where otherwise provided, permission granted in accordance with paragraph (1) of this Article shall not imply permission to record the radio-diffused work by means of instruments recording sounds or images. It shall, however, be a matter for legislation in the countries of the Union to determine the regulations for ephemeral recordings made by a broadcasting body by means of its own facilities and used for its own emissions. The preservation of these recordings in official archives may, on the ground of their exceptional documentary character, be authorised by such legislation.

ARTICLE 11*ter*

Authors of literary works shall enjoy the exclusive right of authorising the public recitation of their works.

ARTICLE 12

Authors of literary, scientific or artistic works shall enjoy the exclusive right of authorising adaptations, arrangements and other alterations of their works.

ARTICLE 13

(1) Authors of musical works shall have the exclusive right of authorising: i. the recording of such works by instruments capable of reproducing them mechanically; ii. the public performance by means of such instruments of works thus recorded.

(2) Reservations and conditions relating to the application of the rights mentioned in the preceding paragraph may be determined by legislation in each country of the Union, in so far as it may be concerned; but all such reservations and conditions shall apply only in the countries which have prescribed them and shall not, in any circumstances, be prejudicial to the author's right to obtain just remuneration which, in the absence of agreement, shall be fixed by competent authority.

(3) The provisions of paragraph (1) of this Article shall not be retroactive and consequently shall not be applicable in a country of the Union to works which, in that country, may have been lawfully adapted to mechanical instruments before the coming into force of the Convention signed at Berlin on the 13th November 1908, and, in the case of a country having acceded to the Convention since that date or acceding to it in the future, before the date of its accession.

(4) Recordings made in accordance with paragraphs (2) and (3) of this Article and imported without permission from the parties concerned into a country where they are not lawfully allowed shall be liable to seizure.

ARTICLE 14

(1) Authors of literary, scientific or artistic works shall have the exclusive right of authorising: i. the cinematographic adaptation and reproduction of these works, and the distribution of the works thus adapted or reproduced; ii. the public presentation and performance of the works thus adapted or reproduced.

(2) Without prejudice to the rights of the author of the work adapted or reproduced, a cinematographic work shall be protected as an original work.

(3) The adaptation under any other artistic form of cinematographic productions derived from literary, scientific or artistic works shall, without prejudice to the authorisation of their authors, remain subject to the authorisation of the author of the original work.

(4) Cinematographic adaptation of literary, scientific or artistic works shall not be subject to the reservations and conditions contained in Article 13, paragraph (2).

(5) The provisions of this Article shall apply to reproduction or production effected by any other process analogous to cinematography.

ARTICLE 14*bis*

(1) The author, or after his death the persons or institutions authorised by national legislation, shall, in respect of original works of art and original manuscripts of writers and composers, enjoy the inalienable right to an interest in any sale of the work subsequent to the first disposal of the work by the author.

(2) The protection provided by the preceding paragraph may be claimed in a country of the Union only if legislation in the country to which the author belongs so permits, and to the degree permitted by the country where this protection is claimed.

(3) The procedure for collection and the amounts shall be matters for determination by national legislation.

ARTICLE 15

(1) In order that the author of a literary or artistic work protected by this Convention shall, in the absence of proof to the contrary, be regarded as such, and consequently be entitled to institute infringement proceedings in countries of the Union, it shall be sufficient for his name to appear on the work in the usual manner. This paragraph shall be applicable even if this name is a pseudonym, where the pseudonym adopted by the author leaves no doubt as to his identity.

(2) In the case of anonymous and pseudonymous works, other than those referred to in the preceding paragraph, the publisher whose name appears on the work shall, in the absence of proof to the contrary, be regarded as representing the author, and in this capacity he shall be entitled to protect and enforce the author's rights. The provisions of this paragraph shall cease to apply if the author reveals his identity and establishes his claim to authorship of the work.

ARTICLE 16

(1) Works infringing copyright may be seized by the competent authorities of any country of the Union where the original work enjoys legal protection.

(2) In these countries the seizure may also apply to reproductions imported from a country where the work is not protected, or has ceased to be protected.

(3) The seizure shall take place in accordance with the legislation of each country.

ARTICLE 17

The provisions of this Convention cannot in any way affect the right of the Government of each country of the Union to permit, to control, or to prohibit by legislation, the circulation, presentation, or exhibition of any work or production in regard to which the competent authority may find it necessary to exercise that right.

ARTICLE 18

(1) This Convention shall apply to all works which at the moment of its coming into force have not yet fallen into the public domain in the country of origin through the expiry of the term of protection.

(2) If, however, through the expiry of the term of protection which was previously granted, a work has fallen into the public domain of the country where protection is claimed, that work shall not be protected anew.

(3) The application of this principle shall be in accordance with the provisions contained in special Conventions to that effect existing or to be concluded between countries of the Union. In the absence of such provisions, the respective countries shall detemine, each in so far as it is concerned, the manner in which the said principle is to be applied.

(4) The above provisions shall apply equally in the case of new accessions to the Union, and in the event of protection being extended by the application of Article 7 or by abandonment of reservations.

ARTICLE 19

The provisions of this Convention shall not preclude the making of a claim to the benefit of any wider provisions which may be afforded by legislation in a country of the Union.

ARTICLE 20

The Governments of the countries of the Union reserve to themselves the right to enter into special Arrangements between each other, in so far as such Arrangements shall confer upon authors more extended rights than those granted by the Convention, or embody other provisions not contrary to this Convention. The provisions of existing Arrangement which satisfy these conditions shall remain applicable.

ARTICLE 21

(1) The International Office established under the name of the "Office of the International Union for the Protection of Literary and Artistic Works" shall be maintained.

(2) That Office shall be placed under the high authority of the Government of the Swiss Confederation, which shall regulate its organisation and supervise its working.

(3) The official language of the Office shall be the French language.

ARTICLE 22

(1) The International Office shall collect information of every kind relating to the protection of the rights of authors over their literary and artistic works. It shall co-ordinate and publish such information. It shall undertake the study of questions of general interest to the Union and, by the aid of documents placed at its disposal by the different Administrations, it shall edit a periodical publication in the French language on questions which concern the purpose of the Union. The Governments of the countries of the Union reserve to themselves the power to authorise by agreement the publication by the Office of an edition in one or more other languages if, by experience, this should be shown to be necessary.

(2) The International Office shall always place itself at the disposal of members of the Union in order to provide them with any special information which they may require relating to the protection of literary and artistic works.

(3) The Director of the International Office shall make an annual report on his administration, which shall be communicated to all the members of the Union.

ARTICLE 23

(1) The expenses of the Office of the International Union shall be shared by the countries of the Union. Until a fresh arrangement is made, they shall not exceed the amount of one hundred and twenty thousand gold francs a year.[6] This amount may be increased, if necessary, by unanimous decision of the countries of the Union or of one of the Conferences provided for in Article 24.

(2) The share of the total expense to be paid by each country shall be determined by the division of the countries of the Union and those subsequently acceding to the Union into six classes, each of which shall contribute in the proportion of a certain number of units, viz.:

1st class	25	units
2nd „	20	„
3rd „	15	„
4th „	10	„
5th „	5	„
6th „	3	„

(3) These coefficients shall be multiplied by the number of countries of each class, and the total product thus obtained will give the number of units by which the total expense is to be divided. The quotient will give the amount of the unit of expense.

(4) Each country shall declare, at the time of its accession, in which of the said classes it desires to be placed, but it may subsequently declare that it wishes to be placed in another class.

(5) The Swiss Administration shall prepare the budget of the Office, supervise its expendi-

[6] This monetary unit is the gold franc of 100 centimes, weighing 10/31 of a gramme and of a fineness of 0.900.

ture, make the necessary advances, and draw up the annual account, which shall be communicated to all the other Administrations.

ARTICLE 24

(1) This Convention may be submitted to revision for the purpose of introducing improvements intended to perfect the system of the Union.

(2) Questions of this kind, as well as those which in other respects concern the development of the Union, shall be considered in Conferences to be held successively in the countries of the Union by delegates of the said countries. The Administration of the country where a Conference is to meet shall, with the assistance of the International Office, prepare the programme of the Conference. The Director of the Office shall attend the sessions of the Conferences, and may take part in the discussions, but without the right to vote.

(3) No alteration in this Convention shall be binding on the Union except by the unanimous consent of the countries composing it.

ARTICLE 25

(1) Countries outside the Union which make provision for the legal protection of the rights forming the object of this Convention may accede thereto upon request.

(2) Such accession shall be notified in writing to the Government of the Swiss Confederation, who shall communicate it to all the other countries of the Union.

(3) Such accession shall imply full acceptance of all the clauses and admission to all the advantages provided by this Convention, and shall take effect one month after the date of the notification made by the Government of the Swiss Confederation to the other countries of the Union, unless some later date has been indicated by the acceding country. It may, nevertheless, contain an indication that the acceding country wishes to substitute, provisionally at least, for Article 8, which relates to translations, the provisions of Article 5 of the Convention of 1886 revised at Paris in 1896, on the understanding that those provisions shall apply only to translations into the langauge or languages of that country.

ARTICLE 26

(1) Any country of the Union may at any time in writing notify the Swiss Government that this Convention shall apply to its overseas territories, colonies, protectorates, territories under its trusteeship, or to any other territory for the international relations of which it is responsible, and the Convention shall thereupon apply to all the territories named in such notification, as from a date determined in accordance with Article 25, paragraph (3). In the absence of such notification, the Convention shall not apply to such territories.

(2) Any country of the Union may at any time in writing notify the Government of the Swiss Confederation that this Convention shall cease to apply to all or any of the territories which have been made the subject of a notification under the preceding paragraph, and the Convention shall cease to apply in the territories named in such notification twelve months after its receipt by the Government of the Swiss Confederation.

(3) All notifications given to the Government of the Swiss Confederation in accordance with the provisions of paragraph (1) and (2) of this Article shall be communicated by that Government to all the countries of the Union.

ARTICLE 27

(1) This convention shall replace, in relations between the countries of the Union, the Convention of Berne of the 9th September 1886, and the subsequent revisions thereof. The Instruments previously in force shall continue to be applicable in relations with countries which do not ratify this Convention.

(2) The countries on whose behalf this Convention is signed may retain the benefit of the reservations which they have previously formulated, on condition that they make declaration to that effect at the time of the deposit of their ratifications.

(3) Countries which are at present members of the Union, but on whose behalf this Convention is not signed, may accede to it at any time, in the manner provided for in Article 25. In that event they shall enjoy the benefit of the provisions of the preceding paragraph.

ARTICLE 27bis

A dispute between two or more countries of the Union concerning the interpretation or application of this Convention, not settled by negotiation, shall be brought before the International Court of Justice for determination by it unless the countries concerned agree on some other method of settlement. The country requesting that the dispute should be brought before the Court shall inform the International Office; the Office shall bring the matter to the attention of the other countries of the Union.

ARTICLE 28

(1) This Convention shall be ratified, and the ratifications deposited at Brussels, not later than the 1st July 1951. The ratifications, with the dates thereof and all declarations which may accompany them, shall be communicated by the Belgian Government to the Government of the Swiss Confederation, which shall notify the other countries of the Union thereof.

(2) This Convention shall come into force, between the countries which have ratified it, one month after the 1st July 1951. Nevertheless, if before that date it has been ratified by at least six countries of the Union, it shall come into force between those countries one month after the notification to them by the Government of the Swiss Confederation of the deposit of the sixth ratification and, in the case of countries which ratify thereafter, one month after the notification of each of such ratifications.

(3) Until the 1st July 1951, countries outside the Union may join it by acceding either to the Convention signed at Rome on the 2nd June 1928, or to this Convention. On or after the 1st July 1951, they may accede only to this Convention. The countries of the Union which shall not have ratified this Convention by the 1st July 1951, may accede thereto in accordance with the procedure provided by Article 25. In this event they shall be entitled to the benefit of the provisions of Article 27, paragraph (2).

ARTICLE 29

(1) This Convention shall remain in force for an indefinite period. Nevertheless, each country of the Union shall be entitled to denounce it at any time by means of a notification in writing addressed to the Government of the Swiss Confederation.

(2) This denunciation, which shall be communicated by the Government of the Swiss Confederation to all the other countries of the Union, shall take effect only in respect of the country making it, and twelve months after the receipt of the notification of denunciation addressed to the Government of the Swiss Confederation. The Convention shall remain in full force and effect for the other countries of the Union.

(3) The right of denunciation provided by this Article shall not be exercised by any country before the expiry of five years from the date of its ratification or accession.

ARTICLE 30

(1) Countries which introduce into their legislation the term of protection of fifty years provided by Article 7, paragraph (1), of this Convention shall give notice thereof in writing to the Government of the Swiss Confederation, which shall immediately communicate it to all the other countries of the Union.

(2) The same procedure shall be followed in the case of countries, abandoning the reservations made or maintained by them in accordance with Articles 25 and 27.

ARTICLE 31

The official Acts of the Conferences shall be established in French. An equivalent text shall be established in English. In case of dispute as to the interpretation of the Acts, the French text shall always prevail. Any country or group of countries of the Union shall be entitled to have established by the International Office an authoritative text of the said Acts in the language of its choice, and by arrangement with the Office. These texts shall be published in the Acts of the Conferences, annexed to the French and English texts.

In faith whereof the respective Plenipotentiaries have signed the Convention.

Done at Brussels, the 26th day of June 1948, in a single copy, which shall be deposited in the archives of the Department of Foreign Affairs and Foreign Trade of Belgium. A copy, duly certified, shall be transmitted by the diplomatic channel to each country of the Union.

[*Here follow the signatures of the Plenipotentiaries of the States (including Australia) on behalf of which the Convention was signed.*]

APPENDIX 3

UNIVERSAL COPYRIGHT CONVENTION
ACCESSIONS AND RATIFICATIONS

As of July 1, 1970*

Country	Effective Date	Country	Effective Date
Andorra	September 16, 1955	Ghana	August 22, 1962
Argentina	February 13, 1958	Greece	August 24, 1963
Australia	May 1, 1969	Guatemala	October 28, 1964
Austria	July 2, 1957	Haiti	September 16, 1955
Belgium	August 31, 1960	Holy See	October 5, 1955
Brazil	January 13, 1960	Iceland	December 18, 1956
Cambodia	September 16, 1955	India	January 21, 1958
Canada	August 10, 1962	Ireland	January 20, 1959
Chile	September 16, 1955	Israel	September 16, 1955
Costa Rica	September 16, 1955	Italy	January 24, 1957
Cuba	June 18, 1957	Japan	April 28, 1956
Czechoslovakia	January 6, 1960	Kenya	September 7, 1966
Denmark	February 9, 1962	Laos	September 16, 1955
Ecuador	June 5, 1957	Lebanon	October 17, 1959
Finland	April 16, 1963	Liberia	July 27, 1956
France	January 14, 1956	Liechtenstein	January 22, 1959
Germany, Federal		Luxembourg	October 15, 1955
Republic of	September 16, 1955	Malawi	October 26, 1965

*Mauritius joined in August 1970 and Hungary in October 1970, bringing the total to sixty countries adhering to the Universal Copyright Convention.

Country	Effective Date	Country	Effective Date
Malta	November 19, 1968	Philippines	November 19, 1955
Mexico	May 12, 1957	Portugal	December 25, 1956
Monaco	September 16, 1955	Spain	September 16, 1955
Netherlands	June 22, 1967	Sweden	July 1, 1961
New Zealand	September 11, 1964	Switzerland	March 30, 1956
Nicaragua	August 16, 1961	Tunisia	June 19, 1969
Nigeria	February 14, 1962	United Kingdom	September 27, 1957
Norway	January 23, 1963	United States	
Pakistan	September 16, 1955	of America	September 16, 1955
Panama	October 17, 1962	Venezuela	September 30, 1966
Paraguay	March 11, 1962	Yugoslavia	May 11, 1966
Peru	October 16, 1963	Zambia	June 1, 1965

APPENDIX 4

UNIVERSAL COPYRIGHT CONVENTION

The Contracting States,

Moved by the desire to assure in all countries copyright protection of literary, scientific and artistic works,

Convinced that a system of copyright protection appropriate to all nations of the world and expressed in a universal convention, additional to, and without impairing international systems already in force, will ensure respect for the rights of the individual and encourage the development of literature, the sciences and the arts,

Persuaded that such a universal copyright system will facilitate a wider dissemination of works of the human mind and increase international understanding,

Have agreed as follows:

ARTICLE I

Each Contracting State undertakes to provide for the adequate and effective protection of the rights of authors and other copyright proprietors in literary, scientific and artistic works, including writings, musical, dramatic and cinematographic works, and paintings, engravings and sculpture.

ARTICLE II

1. Published works of nationals of any Contracting State and works first published in that State shall enjoy in each other Contracting State the same protection as that other State accords to works of its nationals first published in its own territory.

2. Unpublished works of nationals of each Contracting State shall enjoy in each other Contracting State the same protection as that other State accords to unpublished works of its own nationals.

3. For the purpose of this Convention any Contracting State may, by domestic legislation, assimilate to its own nationals any person domiciled in that State.

ARTICLE III

1. Any Contracting State which, under its domestic law, requires as a condition of copyright, compliance with formalities such as deposit, registration, notice, notarial certificates, payment of fees or manufacture or publication in that Contracting State, shall regard these requirements as satisfied with respect to all works protected in accordance with this Convention and first published outside its territory and the author of which is not one of its nationals, if from the time of the first publication all the copies of the work published with the authority of the author or other copyright proprietor bear the symbol © accompanied by the name of the copyright proprietor and the year of first publication placed in such manner and location as to give reasonable notice of claim of copyright.

2. The provisions of paragraph 1 of this Article shall not preclude any Contracting State from requiring formalities or other conditions for the acquisition and enjoyment of copyright in respect of works first published in its territory or works of its nationals wherever published.

3. The provisions of paragraph 1 of this Article shall not preclude any Contracting State from providing that a person seeking judicial relief must, in bringing the action, comply with procedural requirements, such as that the complainant must appear through domestic counsel or that the complainant must deposit with the court or an administrative office, or both, a copy of the work involved in the litigation; provided that failure to comply with such requirements shall not affect the validity of the copyright, nor shall any such requirement be imposed upon a national of another Contracting State if such requirement is not imposed on nationals of the State in which protection is claimed.

4. In each Contracting State there shall be legal means of protecting without formalities the unpublished works of nationals of other Contracting States.

5. If a Contracting State grants protection for more than one term of copyright and the first term is for a period longer than one of the minimum periods prescribed in Article IV, such State shall not be required to comply with the provisions of paragraph 1 of this Article III in respect of the second or any subsequent term of copyright.

ARTICLE IV

1. The duration of protection of a work shall be governed, in accordance with the provisions of Article II and this Article, by the law of the Contracting State in which protection is claimed.

2. The term of protection for works protected under this Convention shall not be less than the life of the author and 25 years after his death.

   However, any Contracting State which, on the effective date of this Convention in that State, has limited this term for certain classes of works to a period computed from the first publication of the work, shall be entitled to maintain these exceptions and to extend them to other classes of works. For all these classes the term of protection shall not be less than 25 years from the date of first publication.

   Any Contracting State which, upon the effective date of this Convention in that State, does not compute the term of protection upon the basis of the life of the author, shall be entitled to compute the term of protection from the date of the first publication of the work or from its registration prior to publication, as the case may be, provided the term of protection shall not be less than 25 years from the date of first publication or from its registration prior to publication, as the case may be.

   If the legislation of a Contracting State grants two or more successive terms of protection, the duration of the first term shall not be less than one of the minimum periods specified above.

3. The provisions of paragraph 2 of this Article shall not apply to photographic works or to works of applied art; provided, however, that the term of protection in those Contracting States which protect photographic works, or works of applied art in so far as they are protected as artistic works, shall not be less than 10 years for each of said classes of works.

4. No Contracting State shall be obliged to grant protection to a work for a period longer than that fixed for the class of works to which the work in question belongs, in the case of unpublished works by the law of the Contracting State of which the author is a national, and in the case of published works by the law of the Contracting State in which the work has been first published.

   For the purposes of the application of the preceding provision, if the law of any Contracting State grants two or more successive terms of protection, the period of protection of that State shall be considered to be the aggregate of those terms. However, if a specified work is not protected by such State during the second or any subsequent term for any reason, the other Contracting States shall not be obliged to protect it during the second or any subsequent term.

5. For the purposes of the application of paragraph 4 of this Article, the work of a national of a Contracting State, first published in a non-Contracting State, shall be treated as though first published in the Contracting State of which the author is a national.

6. For the purposes of the application of paragraph 4 of this Article, in case of simultaneous publication in two or more Contracting States, the work shall be treated as though first published in the State which affords the shortest term; any work published in two or more Contracting States within 30 days of its first publication shall be considered as having been published simultaneously in said Contracting States.

ARTICLE V

1. Copyright shall include the exclusive right of the author to make, publish, and authorize the making and publication of translations of works protected under this Convention.

2. However, any Contracting State may, by its domestic legislation, restrict the right of translation of writings, but only subject to the following provisions:

   If, after the expiration of a period of seven years from the date of the first publication of a writing, a translation of such writing has not been published in the national language or languages, as the case may be, of the Contracting State, by the owner of the right of translation or with his authorization, any national of such Contracting State may obtain a non-exclusive licence from the competent authority thereof to translate the work and publish the work so translated in any of the national languages in which it has not been published; provided that such national, in accordance with the procedure of the State concerned, establishes either that he has requested, and been denied, authorization by the proprietor of the right to make and publish the translation, or that, after due diligence on his part, he was unable to find the owner of the right. A licence may also be granted on the same conditions if all previous editions of a translation in such language are out of print.

   If the owner of the right of translation cannot be found, then the applicant for a licence shall send copies of his application to the publisher whose name appears on the work and, if the nationality of the owner of the right of translation is known, to the diplomatic or consular representative of the State of which such owner is a national, or to the organization which may have been designated by the government of that State. The licence shall not be granted before the expiration of a period of two months from the date of the dispatch of the copies of the application.

   Due provision shall be made by domestic legislation to assure to the owner of the right of translation a compensation which is just and conforms to international standards, to assure payment and transmittal of such compensation, and to assure a correct translation of the work.

The original title and the name of the author of the work shall be printed on all copies of the published translation. The licence shall be valid only for publication of the translation in the territory of the Contracting State where it has been applied for. Copies so published may be imported and sold in another Contracting State if one of the national languages of such other State is the same language as that into which the work has been so translated, and if the domestic law in such other State makes provision for such licences and does not prohibit such importation and sale. Where the foregoing conditions do not exist, the importation and sale of such copies in a Contracting State shall be governed by its domestic law and its agreements. The licence shall not be transferred by the licencee.

The licence shall not be granted when the author has withdrawn from circulation all copies of the work.

ARTICLE VI

"Publication", as used in this Convention, means the reproduction in tangible form and the general distribution to the public of copies of a work from which it can be read or otherwise visually perceived.

ARTICLE VII

This Convention shall not apply to works or rights in works which, at the effective date of the Convention in a Contracting State where protection is claimed, are permanently in the public domain in the said Contracting State.

ARTICLE VIII

1. This Convention, which shall bear the date of 6 September 1952, shall be deposited with the Director-General of the United Nations Educational, Scientific and Cultural Organization and shall remain open for signature by all States for a period of 120 days after that date. It shall be subject to ratification or acceptance by the signatory States.

2. Any State which has not signed this Convention may accede thereto.

3. Ratification, acceptance or accession shall be effected by the deposit of an instrument to that effect with the Director-General of the United Nations Educational, Scientific and Cultural Organization.

ARTICLE IX

1. This Convention shall come into force three months after the deposit of twelve instruments of ratification, acceptance or accession, among which there shall be those of four States which are not members of the International Union for the Protection of Literary and Artistic Works.

2. Subsequently, this Convention shall come into force in respect of each State three months after that State has deposited its instrument of ratification, acceptance or accession.

ARTICLE X

1. Each State party to this Convention undertakes to adopt, in accordance with its Constitution, such measures as are necessary to ensure the application of this Convention.

2. It is understood, however, that at the time an instrument of ratification, acceptance or accession is deposited on behalf of any State, such State must be in a position under its domestic law to give effect to the terms of this Convention.

ARTICLE XI

1. An Inter-governmental Committee is hereby established with the following duties:

   (a) to study the problems concerning the application and operation of this Convention;

   (b) to make preparation for periodic revisions of this Convention;

   (c) to study any other problems concerning the international protection of copyright, in co-operation with the various interested international organizations, such as the United Nations Educational, Scientific and Cultural Organization, the International Union for the Protection of Literary and Artistic Works and the Organization of American States;

   (d) to inform the Contracting States as to its activities.

2. The Committee shall consist of the representatives of twelve Contracting States to be selected with due consideration to fair geographical representation and in conformity with the Resolution relating to this article, annexed to this Convention.

   The Director-General of the United Nations Educational, Scientific and Cultural Organization, the Director of the Bureau of the International Union for the Protection of Literary and Artistic Works and the Secretary-General of the Organization of American States, or their representatives, may attend meetings of the Committee in an advisory capacity.

ARTICLE XII

The Inter-governmental Committee shall convene a conference for revision of this Convention whenever it deems necessary, or at the request of at least ten Contracting States, or of a majority of the Contracting States if there are less than twenty Contracting States.

ARTICLE XIII

Any Contracting State may, at the time of deposit of its instrument of ratification, acceptance or accession, or at any time thereafter declare by notification addressed to the Director-General of the United Nations Educational, Scientific and Cultural Organization that this Convention shall apply to all or any of the countries or territories for the international relations of which it is responsible and this Convention shall thereupon apply to the countries or territories named in such notification after the expiration of the term of three months provided for in Article IX. In the absence of such notification, this Convention shall not apply to any such country or territory.

ARTICLE XIV

1. Any Contracting State may denounce this Convention in its own name or on behalf of all or any of the countries or territories as to which a notification has been given under Article XIII. The denunciation shall be made by notification addressed to the Director-General of the United Nations Educational, Scientific and Cultural Organization.

2. Such denunciation shall operate only in respect of the State or of the country or territory on whose behalf it was made and shall not take effect until twelve months after the date of receipt of the notification.

ARTICLE XV

A dispute between two or more Contracting States concerning the interpretation or application of this Convention, not settled by negotiation, shall, unless the States concerned agree on some other method of settlement, be brought before the International Court of Justice for determination by it.

ARTICLE XVI

1. This Convention shall be established in English, French and Spanish. The three texts shall be signed and shall be equally authoritative.

2. Official texts of this Convention shall be established in German, Italian and Portuguese.

   Any Contracting State or group of Contracting States shall be entitled to have established by the Director-General of the United Nations Educational, Scientific and Cultural Organization other texts in the language of its choice by arrangement with the Director General.

   All such texts shall be annexed to the signed texts of this Convention.

ARTICLE XVII

1. This Convention shall not in any way affect the provisions of the Berne Convention for the Protection of Literary and Artistic Works or membership in the Union created by that Convention.

2. In application of the foregoing paragraph, a Declaration has been annexed to the present article. This Declaration is an integral part of this Convention for the States bound by the Berne Convention on January 1, 1951, or which have or may become bound to it at a later date. The signature of this Convention by such States shall also constitute signature of the said Declaration, and ratification, acceptance or accession by such States shall include the Declaration as well as the Convention.

ARTICLE XVIII

This Convention shall not abrogate multilateral or bilateral copyright conventions or arrangements that are or may be in effect exclusively between two or more American Republics. In the event of any difference either between the provisions of such existing conventions or arrangements and the provisions of this Convention, or between the provisions of this Convention and those of any new convention or arrangement which may be formulated between two or more American Republics after this Convention comes into force, the convention or arrangement most recently formulated shall prevail between the parties thereto. Rights in works acquired in any Contracting State under existing conventions or arrangements before the date this Convention comes into force in such State shall not be affected.

ARTICLE XIX

This Convention shall not abrogate multilateral or bilateral conventions or arrangements in effect between two or more Contracting States. In the event of any difference between the provisions of such existing conventions or arrangements and the provisions of this Convention, the provisions of this Convention shall prevail. Rights in works acquired in any Contracting State under existing conventions or arrangements before the date on which this Convention comes into force in such State shall not be affected. Nothing in this article shall affect the provisions of Articles XVII and XVIII of this Convention.

ARTICLE XX

Reservations to this Convention shall not be permitted.

ARTICLE XXI

The Director-General of the United Nations Educational, Scientific and Cultural Organization shall send duly certified copies of this Convention to the States interested, to the Swiss Federal Council and the Secretary-General of the United Nations for registration by him.

   He shall also inform all interested States of the ratifications, acceptances and accessions which have been deposited, the date on which this Convention comes into force, the notifications under Article XIII of this Convention, and denunciations under Article XIV.

APPENDIX DECLARATION RELATING TO ARTICLE XVII

The States which are members of the International Union for the Protection of Literary and Artistic Works, and which are signatories to the Universal Copyright Convention,

Desiring to reinforce their mutual relations on the basis of the said Union and to avoid any conflict which might result from the co-existence of the Convention of Berne and the Universal Convention,

Have, by common agreement, accepted the terms of the following declaration:

(a) Works which, according to the Berne Convention, have as their country of origin a country which has withdrawn from the International Union created by the said Convention, after January 1, 1951, shall not be protected by the Universal Copyright Convention in the countries of the Berne Union;

(b) The Universal Copyright Convention shall not be applicable to the relationships among countries of the Berne Union insofar as it relates to the protection of works having as their country of origin, within the meaning of the Berne Convention, a country of the International Union created by the said Convention.

RESOLUTION CONCERNING ARTICLE XI

The Inter-governmental Copyright Conference

Having considered the problems relating to the Inter-governmental Committee provided for in Article XI of the Universal Copyright Convention,

resolves

1. The first members of the Committee shall be representatives of the following twelve States, each of those States designating one representative and an alternate: Argentina, Brazil, France, Germany, India, Italy, Japan, Mexico, Spain, Switzerland, United Kingdom, and United States of America.

2. The Committee shall be constituted as soon as the Convention comes into force in accordance with Article XI of this Convention.

3. The Committee shall elect its chairman and one vice-chairman. It shall establish its rules of procedure having regard to the following principles:

   (a) the normal duration of the term of office of the representatives shall be six years; with one-third retiring every two years;

   (b) before the expiration of the term of office of any members, the Committee shall decide which States shall cease to be represented on it and which States shall be called upon to designate representatives; the representatives of those States which have not ratified, accepted or acceded shall be the first to retire;

   (c) the different parts of the world shall be fairly represented;
and expresses the wish
that the United Nations Educational, Scientific and Cultural Organization provide its secretariat.

In faith whereof the undersigned, having deposited their respective full powers, have signed this Convention.

Done at Geneva, this sixth day of September, 1952 in a single copy.

Protocol 1

Annexed to the Universal Copyright Convention concerning the application of that Convention to the works of stateless persons and refugees

The States parties hereto, being also parties to the Universal Copyright Convention (hereinafter referred to as the "Convention"),

Have accepted the following provisions:

1. Stateless persons and refugees who have their habitual residence in a State party to this Protocol shall, for the purposes of the Convention, be assimilated to the nationals of that State.

2. (a) This Protocol shall be signed and shall be subject to ratification or acceptance, or may be acceded to, as if the provisions of Article VIII of the Convention applied hereto.

   (b) This Protocol shall enter into force in respect of each State, on the date of deposit of the instrument of ratification, acceptance or accession of the State concerned or on the date of entry into force of the Convention with respect to such State, whichever is the later.

In faith whereof the undersigned, being duly authorized thereto, have signed this Protocol.

Done at Geneva this sixth day of September, 1952, in the English, French and Spanish languages, the three texts being equally authoritative, in a single copy which shall be deposited with the Director-General of Unesco. The Director-General shall send certified copies to the signatory States, to the Swiss Federal Council, and to the Secretary-General of the United Nations for registration.

Protocol 2

Annexed to the Universal Copyright Convention, concerning the application of that Convention to the works of certain international organizations

The States parties hereto, being also parties to the Universal Copyright Convention (hereinafter referred to as the "Convention"),

Have accepted the following provisions:

1. (a) The protection provided for in Article II(1) of the Convention shall apply to works published for the first time by the United Nations, by the Specialized Agencies in relationship therewith, or by the Organization of American States;

   (b) Similarly, Article II(2) of the Convention shall apply to the said organization or agencies.

2. (a) This Protocol shall be signed and shall be subject to ratification or acceptance, or may be acceded to, as if the provisions of Article VIII of the Convention applied hereto.

   (b) This Protocol shall enter into force for each State on the date of deposit of the instrument of ratification, acceptance or accession of the State concerned or on the date of entry into force of the Convention with respect to such State, whichever is the later.

In faith whereof the undersigned, being duly authorized thereto, have signed this Protocol.

Done at Geneva, this sixth day of September, 1952, in the English, French and Spanish languages, the three texts being equally authoritative, in a single copy which shall be deposited with the Director-General of Unesco.

The Director-General shall send certified copies to the signatory States, to the Swiss Federal Council, and to the Secretary-General of the United Nations for registration.

Protocol 3

Annexed to the Universal Copyright Convention concerning the effective date of instruments of ratification or acceptance of or accession to that Convention

States parties hereto,

Recognizing that the application of the Universal Copyright Convention (hereinafter referred to as the "Convention") to States participating in all the international copyright systems already in force will contribute greatly to the value of the Convention;

Have agreed as follows:

1. Any State party hereto may, on depositing its instrument of ratification or acceptance of or accession to the Convention, notify the Director-General of the United Nations Educational, Scientific and Cultural Organization (hereinafter referred to as "Director-General") that that instrument shall not take effect for the purposes of Article IX of the Convention until any other State named in such notification shall have deposited its instrument.

2. The notification referred to in paragraph 1 above shall accompany the instrument to which it relates.

3. The Director-General shall inform all States signatory or which have then acceded to the Convention of any notifications received in accordance with this Protocol.

4. This Protocol shall bear the same date and shall remain open for signature for the same period as the Convention.

5. It shall be subject to ratification or acceptance by the signatory States. Any State which has not signed this Protocol may accede thereto.

6. (a) Ratification or acceptance or accession shall be effected by the deposit of an instrument to that effect with the Director-General.

   (b) This Protocol shall enter into force on the date of deposit of not less than four instruments of ratification or acceptance or accession. The Director-General shall inform all interested States of this date. Instruments deposited after such date shall take effect on the date of their deposit.

In faith whereof the undersigned, being duly authorized thereto, have signed this Protocol.

Done at Geneva, the sixth day of September 1952, in the English, French and Spanish languages, the three texts being equally authoritative, in a single copy which shall be annexed to the original copy of the Convention. The Director-General shall send certified copies to the signatory States, to the Swiss Federal Council, and to the Secretary-General of the United Nations for registration.

REFERENCES

1. U.S. Congress, Senate Committee on Foreign Relations, *Executive Report No. 5,* June 11, 1954.
2. A. Goldman, "The History of U.S.A. Copyright Law Revision from 1901 to 1954" in *Studies on Copyright,* Vol. II, Part IX, Rothman, New Jersey, 1963, p. 3.
3. Presentation by Senator Hickenlooper to the Senate on June 25, 1954, Ref. 2 , p. 14.

WILLIAM Z. NASRI

Copyright as It Affects Libraries: Legal Implications*

I. PHILOSOPHICAL BASES OF COPYRIGHT

Copyright has two faces, both of which bear features that should stir a feeling of fellowship in librarians. Both are reflected in the clause of the Constitution, on which the copyright law is founded, empowering Congress

> To promote the Progress of Science and useful Arts, by securing for limited Times to Authors and Inventors the exclusive Right to their respective Writings and Discoveries.

One face of copyright looks squarely at authors—among whom are composers and artists as well as writers—and recognizes that their works contribute immeasurably to man's knowledge and to the quality of human life. It sees, with Supreme Court Justice Reed (in *Mazer* v. *Stein,* 347 U.S. 201, 219), that

> The economic philosophy behind the clause empowering Congress to grant patents and copyrights is the conviction that encouragement of individual effort by personal gain is the best way to advance public welfare through the talents of authors and inventors in 'Science and useful Arts'. Sacrificial days devoted to such creative activities deserve rewards commensurate with the service rendered.

It sees, moreover, that if authors are to devote their time and talents to creating works of literature, music, and art, they must be given the opportunity to derive compensation, as well as a measure of honor, from those who use and enjoy their works.

This face of copyright looks also at publishers and other processors who transform and package the works of authors so as to present them to the public. And it sees that they must be afforded the economic returns that will enable them to perform their functions.

In essence, copyright is a legal device designed to provide the opportunity for economic reward that enables authors to expend their energies in creation, and enables publishers to invest their resources and efforts in making the authors' works available to the public. Copyright seeks to achieve this end by giving to authors, who in turn may grant to publishers or other producers, broad rights of control over the various modes of reproduction of their works, or, at least, the right to exact payment for their reproduction.

Other means of supporting authorship and publication—including private patronage, institutional grants, and government subvention—have been known and are still used in special situations, particularly for esoteric works that have no substantial commercial market. But they have serious short-comings and narrowly limited areas of usefulness. Reliance upon the market place, where those who receive the benefit of using a work are called upon to pay for it, has been the underlying principle of copyright, and has proved the best means so far devised to achieve the

---

*The views expressed in this article are those of the author individually and do not necessarily reflect the views of the Copyright Office.

purpose of stimulating the creation and publication of the wide range and volume of authorial works.

Librarians, because they appreciate the value to society of works of authorship and play a major part in the process of disseminating those works, can feel the close kinship of their own role with those of authors and publishers.

At the same time, the other visage of copyright perceives that the social value of works of authorship ("the progress of Science and useful Arts") lies in their use by the public for its education, cultural enrichment, and diversion. In the direct view of this visage are the scholar and researcher, the teacher and student, and the mass of people making up the reading, listening, and viewing public. In its peripheral view are other users, including the various media of public dissemination; and here we see again, from another angle, publishers and even authors who must learn from their predecessors.

Contemplating these groups of users makes one aware that it is not enough to have copyright stimulate the production of works of authorship; it must also foster the dissemination of those works and their availability for use. The rights of control accorded to authors by copyright must therefore be tempered accordingly to avoid any undue restrictions on the use of their works.

Librarians can readily see their role as intermediaries between the producers and users of works, and they may well refer to their services in making works accessible to users as the end purpose of libraries.

The core problem of copyright is how best to merge these two aspects: first, providing the reward due to the creators of intellectual works, and the concomitant economic support required by the packagers and distributors of those works; and second, facilitating the public's access to and use of them. At about the same time that the Constitution was being written, Lord Mansfield, the famous English judge, stated the problem this way (in *Sayre* v. *Moore,* 102 Eng. Rep. 139):

> We must take care to guard against two extremes equally prejudicial; the one, that men of ability, who have employed their time for the service of the community, may not be deprived of their just merits, and the reward of their ingenuity and labour; the other, that the world may not be deprived of improvements, nor the progress of the arts be retarded.

So it is that most countries of the world have copyright laws that seek to stimulate creative authorship and the public availability of intellectual works. The laws vary in detail from one country to another; thus, the scope of the rights accorded to authors to control or demand compensation for the use of their works may vary with the esteem in which authors are regarded, or with the relative emphasis placed on cultural and material values; or may vary with the general level of the country's economic and social development, or more specifically with the national volume of its domestic production and of its imports and exports of works of authorship, or with the literacy rate. (It must be acknowledged that the United States, under its present copyright law, is less generous toward authors than most other major countries.) While these differences are significant, however, more important to the whole picture is the basic approach common to copyright laws the world over: for the end purpose of fostering the growth and spread of learning and culture, authors are given legal rights in the reproduction of the works they create so that they may derive the rewards afforded by the market for their works, but those rights are kept within limits as necessary to facilitate the use of their works by the public.

II. POSTURE OF THE U.S. LAW

Exercising the power explicitly granted by the Constitution, the First Congress enacted the first copyright statute of the United States in 1790, patterning it after the original English copyright statute of 1710 and the similar acts that had been adopted by 12 of the 13 newly independent states during the 1780s. Aside from numerous amendments on particular points over the years, the U.S. Statute of 1790 was completely rewritten three times at intervals of about 40 years—in 1831, 1870, and 1909. The Act of 1909, with only minor amendments, is still the law today, 60 years later.

In view of the radical technological innovations and the changes in the economic structure since 1909, it has been universally recognized that another complete revision of the copyright law is overdue. It need only be recalled that since 1909 have come wholly new complexes of mass communication by radio, television, and wire systems, as well as revolutionary improvements in visual and sound recording and in reproduction techniques; and the problems of adapting the copyright law to the new electronic era have very recently been posed most acutely—though they are not yet seen in clear focus—by the prospective development of computer-based systems in which entire libraries of copyrighted works will be stored and made available for reproduction and transmission on demand.

Beginning in 1955 the Copyright Office, under Congressional authorization, conducted a program of studies, conferences, and discussions of proposals for a general revision of the copyright law, which led to the introduction of a general revision bill in Congress in 1965 (H.R. 4347 and S. 1006, 89th Cong.). After extensive hearings and extraordinarily thorough consideration in committee, the revision bill in amended form (H.R. 2512, 90th Cong.) was passed by the House of Representatives on April 11, 1967. It has since been pending (now S. 543, 91st Cong.) in the Senate Subcommittee with some prospect of Senate action in the present (91st) Congress.

Because the problems concerning the use of copyrighted works in computer-based information systems are not yet understood sufficiently for legislative resolution, a bill (S. 2216, 90th Cong.) was passed by the Senate on October 12, 1967, to establish a National Commission on New Technological Uses of Copyrighted Works, which would study those problems and submit its recommendations within three years. The House of Representatives took no action on this bill. The entire text of the Commission bill has been appended to the general revision bill as part of S. 543 now pending in the 91st Congress.

III. WORKS SUBJECT TO COPYRIGHT

A. *Categories of Copyrightable Works*

As a broad generality, copyright can be said to embrace works of creative authorship of all kinds—literary, musical, graphic, and artistic. The present U.S. copyright law enumerates, more specifically, thirteen classes of works that are eligible for copyright (17 U.S. Code §5). As might be expected, this enumeration reads much like a list of the materials to be found in the collections of a comprehensive library;

(a) Books, including composite and cyclopedic works, directories, gazetteers, and other compilations.
(b) Periodicals, including newspapers.
(c) Lectures, sermons, addresses (prepared for oral delivery).
(d) Dramatic or dramatico-musical compositions.
(e) Musical compositions.
(f) Maps.
(g) Works of art; models or designs for works of art.
(h) Reproductions of a work of art.
(i) Drawings or plastic works of a scientific or technical character.
(j) Photographs.
(k) Prints and pictorial illustrations including prints or labels used for articles of merchandise.
(l) Motion-picture photoplays.
(m) Motion pictures other than photoplays.

The pending bill for revision of the copyright law (S. 543, 91st Cong.) covers all of the kinds of works comprised in the present law, but does so under a different list of six categories:

(1) literary works;
(2) musical works, including any accompanying words;
(3) dramatic works, including any accompanying music;
(4) pantomimes and choreographic works;
(5) pictorial, graphic, and sculptural works;
(6) motion pictures and other audio-visual works;

and adds a new seventh category:

(7) sound recordings.

This new category would extend copyright protection to the rendition fixed in, and reproducible from, the particular recording, as distinguished from the musical or literary work of which the rendition is recorded.

B. *Manuscripts*

As long as a work remains unpublished, it is protected by the common law as the literary property of the author and his heirs, with no time limit (except that, for the kinds of works that are commonly performed or exhibited without being published—lectures, music, dramas, pictorial and art works—the author may secure copyright under the statute, if he wishes, by a voluntary registration). Underlying the author's common law rights are considerations of privacy as well as the usual considerations of property. Since common law protection continues indefinitely (until the work is published or registered), libaries and archives holding manuscript collections are faced with questions concerning the availability of their manuscripts for copying, publication, or other use.

Where manuscripts are acquired from the authors or their heirs, it is possible to make arrangements with them for uses of the manuscripts; but otherwise the possibility remains that, even for manuscripts of considerable age, the author's heirs may assert their literary property rights. The problem becomes more evident when it is recalled that the literary property in letters belongs to the writer and his heirs, while it is commonly the recipient or his heirs who places letters in a library's manuscript collection. As a practical matter, of course, the likelihood of an author's heirs asserting their literary property rights diminishes with the age of the manuscript, and ultimately becomes negligible. But how long is "ultimate"?

The revision bill would change the situation regarding manuscripts. It would extend protection under the copyright statute to all copyrightable works from the time of their creation; the rights of authors and their heirs in unpublished works would then be governed by the statute instead of the common law. The most important consequence would be that all rights in manuscripts would terminate at the end of the copyright term—50 years after the author's death—whereupon they would be in the public domain. (Because of Constitutional considerations, rights in existing manuscripts would be continued for at least 25 years after the new law takes effect.)

The revision bill also contains another innovation regarding manuscripts in the collections of nonprofit archival institutions. It would explicitly permit any such institutions to make facsimile copies of unpublished works in its collections "for purposes of preservation and security, or for deposit for research use in any other such institution."

Whatever the law allows with respect to the use of manuscripts, libraries would still be obligated, of course, to abide by any restrictions that the donors of manuscripts impose upon their use as a condition of their deposit.

C. Published Works

1. Copyright Notice. Under the present statute, copyright is secured by publishing copies of the work bearing a prescribed notice of copyright. This notice consists of the word "Copyright" or the abbreviation "Copr." or the symbol © (C in a circle), together with the name of the copyright owner and, for most works, the year date of first publication.

If copies of a work are published without the copyright notice, users are generally entitled to assume that the work is in the public domain. If a published work does bear the notice, it should usually be assumed that the work (or at least such parts as are not known to be in the public domain) are protected until the copyright term expires.

When a work contains both material in the public domain and copyrightable new matter—for example, a nineteenth century novel with a new introduction—, the copyright reflected by the notice covers only the new matter, whether the notice so indicates or not.

Librarians, as well as educational and other groups of users of copyrighted material, have stated that the copyright notice is of great value to them. It serves both as a convenient source of information about the copyright status of the work, and as an indication, given by the year date, of its recency; the year date is said to be particularly useful in works that appear in successive editions.

Although the United States is virtually alone in the world in requiring a copyright notice on published copies, the revision bill would continue to require the notice in view of its value to libraries and others. However, because many copyrights have been lost under the present law by inadvertent omission of the notice, the revision bill would relax the present stringency of the notice requirement. The bill would allow the copyright owner to preserve his copyright, where the notice had been omitted, by registering his copyright claim. Nevertheless, anyone who acts in good faith in reliance upon the absence of the notice, and thereby infringes innocently, would still be shielded from liability for the infringement.

2. Deposit and Registration. Most countries have some legal requirement that copies of works published domestically be deposited in their national libraries. In the United States, the copyright statute calls for the deposit in the Copyright Office of two copies (or one copy or a substitute in special cases) of every work published with a notice of copyright. The deposit is accompanied by an application and fee for registration of the copyright.

Aside from serving to identify the work for which copyright is registered, the deposit copies are available to the Library of Congress for addition to its collections or for exchange with other libraries. A substantial part of the acquisitions of the Library of Congress comes from copyright deposits.

The Library of Congress does not take all the deposits received in the Copyright Office. Among the deposited articles are such items, not wanted by the library, as advertising matter, trade catalogs, toys, jewelry, and a miscellany of ephemera. During the 1969 fiscal year, for example, out of a total of about 476,000 articles deposited, the library took about 293,000, or slightly over 60%.

The Copyright Office issues semiannual printed catalogs of all the works it registers. The catalogs are issued in several parts for different classes of works, and they are supplied to depository libraries throughout the United States as well as being offered for sale to the public. Many persons have found them valuable sources of information, not only about the copyright in particular works, but also for general bibliographic data.

D. The Public Domain

A work in the public domain is, by definition, free of any copyright restrictions; it is available for reproduction or any other use by everyone. Once in the public domain, a work cannot thereafter be made subject to copyright.

A work may be in the public domain by virtue of its publication without a notice of copyright, or because of the expiration of the copyright. Also in the public domain, by express statutory declaration (17 U.S.C. §8), is any "publication of the United States Government."

1. Publication without Notice. It has already been noted that publication of a work without the prescribed copyright notice will generally place the work in the public domain. It should be added, however, that there are exceptional situations in which copyright subsists though copies of the work do not bear the notice. Thus, when copies are distributed to a limited group of persons for a special purpose—e.g., to several of the author's friends for their comments—, the work is not thereby "published" (but such copies are not likely to find their way into libraries). Another instance is that of unauthorized copies, which may not always be recognized as such; the copyright owner, of course, is not responsible for their issuance without a notice.

2. Expiration of Copyright. Under the present law, copyright in the United States expires either 28 or 56 years after the date of first publication of the work, depending upon whether the copyright was renewed, by filing for renewal in the Copyright Office, before the end of the first 28-year term. (By a series of special legislative enactments, however, all copyrights that began between September 19, 1906 and December 31, 1915 and were later renewed, have been extended beyond the usual 56-year period to endure until December 31, 1971. This series of extensions anticipates enactment of the general revision bill under which the total term of existing copyrights, if renewed, would be 75 instead of 56 years from first publication.)

One of the most important features of the revision bill would be to change the duration of copyright in the United States to correspond with the term most prevalent in other countries. Our present term of 28 years from publication of the work plus a renewal for another 28 years is unique and, in view of the growing importance of worldwide distribution and transmission of works of authorship, is generally considered an anachronism. Almost all other countries have a copyright term running for the life of the author and a period of years after his death; most commonly this post-mortem period is 50 years, and this is the period required for adherence to the most important international copyright convention, that of the Berne Union.

The revision bill would adopt, for works created in the future, the basic term of the author's life and 50 years after his death. There are some situations, however, in which the term cannot be measured from the author's death: in this category are anonymous works and works of corporate authorship. For these works the revision bill provides for a term of 75 years from first publication, or 100 years from creation of the work, whichever expires first.

Since it is anticipated that it may often be difficult, and sometimes impossible, to ascertain when a little-known author died, the revision bill has a special provision to meet this problem. The Copyright Office would keep records of the deaths of authors; and after the lapse of 75 years from first publication or 100 years from creation of a work, if the Copyright Office could not supply information to the contrary, a user could act on the assumption that the author has been dead for 50 years.

3. U.S. Government Publications. The United States Government produces and distributes, to depository libraries among others, a large volume of official documents and reports and general informational material. Works produced by the U.S. Government are excluded from copyright by express provision of the statute.

A word of caution needs to be added here. The government reproduces and publishes some privately copyrighted material, and the fact of its publication by the government does not affect the copyright.

Material produced by state and local governmental bodies (other than official legal documents) are copyrightable, and some of this material is protected by copyright as evidenced by a copyright notice on the published copies.

IV. USES OF COPYRIGHTED WORKS

A. General Observations

The essence of copyright is that authors are given exclusive rights to make certain uses of the works they create. But copyright does not extend to all uses of works. The copyright statute spells out the uses to which authors are given exclusive rights, and imposes certain limits on those rights.

Uses other than those specified in the statute are not subject to copyright. Some simple illustrations are the reading or reciting of a work privately, or the loan or gift or sale of one's copy of a work to another person, or the use of information gained from the work.

Regarding the use of information, it is a basic concept of copyright that the knowledge or ideas imparted by a work are freely available to everyone to make use of, even if the author is disclosing a discovery or novel thought of his own. For the advancement of learning, writers, scholars, and researchers must gather information and ideas from the works of their predecessors. What copyright protects is the author's individual expression of ideas in words or music or pictures of his own creation, or his own collection and arrangement of factual information. Anyone else is free to write about the same subject matter or theme, or to express the same thought or convey the same information in a work of his own creation. So it is, for example, that a historian or biographer may report, in his own work, facts and incidents derived from earlier histories or biographies that are under copyright. Similarly, practical ideas disclosed by a work—how to do something—may be put into practice by anyone, though the author's individual way of explaining how to do it is protected by copyright.

B. Uses Controlled by Copyright

1. Reproduction and Distribution. Of the uses to which the author (or his successor as the copyright owner) is given the exclusive rights, the most basic are the making and distribution of copies of the work. As to books, periodicals, and other works that are disseminated by the distribution of copies, the main source of revenue for authors and publishers is the sale of copies; and in a broad sense, the copyright law is designed to protect the copyright owner against the unauthorized making by others of copies that might otherwise have been sold by him.

The copying that infringes copyright is not confined to exact and complete duplication of the work. Reproduction of an essential portion may be an infringement; as may be also an imitative reproduction of the substance of the work, though disguised by alterations. And the author's exclusive rights extend to the re-creation of his work in a different version, such as a translation of his original text, a dramatization of his novel, or an adaptation of his musical composition.

2. Public Performance. The copyright owner of a dramatic work or of a motion picture has the exclusive right to perform the work for a public audience. The similar right in nondramatic literary and music works is limited to public performance "for profit"; any element of commercial purpose will make a performance one "for profit," but wholly noncommercial performance of such works—for example, a free concert given by a school band, or the reading of stories by a librarian to a group of children—are excluded from copyright.

The copyright revision bill would make one significant change here. As a consequence of the "for profit" limitation, the authors of nondramatic musical and literary works now receive nothing for the performances of their works by noncommercial radio and television broadcasting stations, although their broadcasts reach a vast audience and are a principal medium for the public performance of contemporary "serious" music and literature. The revision bill would extend the author's right of public performance to non-commercial broadcasting (except for systematic instructional broadcasts by and for nonprofit educational institutions).

3. Televisual Display. The revision bill would also deal with another related question that has been brought to the fore by television and is shrouded in uncertainty under the present law: the bill specifies that the author's rights extend to the display of his work in television transmissions to the public. Televisual displays are a matter of particular significance with respect to pictorial and other art works; and they may assume importance in the future for textual material if such displays are so made that, through sustained and repeated images of the text, they serve the functions of copies.

The bill states explicitly that the owner of a copy of a work—e.g., a library—would be entitled to display it for viewing by the public at the place where the copy is located (as distinguished from display of its image in a television transmission).

C. Reproduction of Works in Libraries

The copyright question that has aroused the greatest interest among librarians concerns the "photocopying" (in the broad sense of any kind of machine reproduction) of copyrighted material in a library's collections for anyone requesting a copy. This question has usually been considered in the context of the doctrine of "fair use."

1. Fair Use in General. The doctrine of fair use has been called the "safety valve" of copyright, and it is one of the most important elements in maintaining the balance between the two aims of the copyright law: to give authors their just reward, but also to make their works available to the public for beneficial use. Stated very simply—too simply to serve as a reliable definition—the doctrine of fair use permits the reproduction, for legitimate purposes, of material taken from a copyrighted work to a limited extent that will not cut into the copyright owner's potential market for the sale of copies.

Fair use cannot be defined in precise terms; it may apply in an endless variety of circumstances for many purposes, and there is no mathematical formula as to how much of a work may be reproduced for any particular purpose. It calls for reasonable judgment in much the same way as such imprecise concepts as "good faith" or "ethical conduct." It has been suggested that a good pragmatic test of fair use might be to ask oneself: if I were the author or publisher of this work, would I think that this particular use of it without my permission is fair?

The doctrine of fair use has been developed by the courts, over many years, in a variety of situations. For the most part, the court decisions have dealt with cases in which a part of one author's work was quoted by another writer. Quotation has been held to be fair use when made to a reasonable extent for purposes such as review or criticism, or to illustrate or emphasize a point. Until recently, the courts had not been called upon to consider the fair use doctrine specifically in the context of library photocopying; but this precise question is involved in a suit now pending in the U.S. Court of Claims (*The Williams and Wilkins Co.* v. *The United States*) in which the plaintiff charges that its copyrights in several medical journals have been infringed by the photocopying of articles from those journals by the National Library of Medicine.

The copyright revision bill would affirm the fair use doctrine expressly, and it sets forth the main factors, distilled from the court decisions, for determining what is a fair use. These factors are: (1) the purpose and character of the use; (2) the nature of the copyrighted work; (3) the amount and substantiality of the portion used in relation to the copyrighted work as a whole; and (4) the effect of the use upon the potential market for or value of the copyrighted work.

A few simple examples may throw some light on the application of these factors in practice. The revision bill itself mentions, as examples of purposes for which fair use of a work may be made, "criticism, comment, news reporting, teaching, scholarship, or research."

With respect to the nature of the work, extracting informational passages from technical works, for example, would be easier to justify than copying an act from a play; for another example, there would usually be less reason, for purposes of research, to copy musical scores or photographs than to copy textual material.

As for amount and substantiality, it would be relatively easy to justify copying two pages from a 100-page treatise (except, perhaps, where those two pages were the entire summary and conclusion, and therefore the very core of the treatise); but relatively difficult to justify copying fifty of the 100 pages, especially where copies were available for purchase.

2. The Bases for Library Photocopying. The doctrine of fair use is commonly cited as a basis for justifying the making of single copies of material in libraries for purposes of research and study. As already indicated, the extent to which library photocopying may be permitted as a fair use has not been adjudicated by the courts. But commentators have presented the rationale that the making of a single copy of a reasonable portion of a work for private reference use is within the framework of the recognized criteria of fair use.

Running parallel with the fair use doctrine is the longstanding and accepted custom whereby scholars have felt free to copy by hand any excerpts they wished to have as notes for their reference use. It is argued that making a copy for the same purpose by a photocopying device is equally justified, and that scholars should not be denied the labor-saving benefit of modern devices.

Photocopying, however, has complicated the problem. What the scholar could copy by hand was inherently limited by the process itself; he would rarely copy the whole of a lengthy work, and he was not likely to make more than one copy. Photocopying machines have made it easy to copy extensively and in multiple copies. Instead of being merely a labor-saving substitute for hand copying, these machines are now capable of substituting for the printing press, and their use for multiple reproduction may become part of the process of publishing. Copyright owners have expressed the fear that photocopying may get out of hand to such an extent as to compete with the potential market for regularly published copies.

On behalf of libraries and scholarly and research organizations, it has been urged that the library's function is to provide materials for research; that the needs of researchers for library materials cannot be met effectively through loans; and that researchers should be able to enjoy the benefits of modern copying techniques.

On the basis of such considerations, a group of research organizations and an association of publishers reached what was called a "gentlemen's agreement" in 1935. This was not, in fact, a binding agreement, but it indicates the thinking on both sides at that time. The gentlemen's agreement stated, in substance, that a library could make a single photocopy of a part of a book or periodical volume in its collections for delivery to a scholar who represented in writing that he desired the photocopy in lieu of a loan, or in place of manual transcription, and solely for the purpose of research.

In 1941 the American Library Association adopted a statement of policy for its members, which accepted the substance of the gentlemen's agreement.

Since that time, all concerned have become more acutely aware of the problem, as copying machines have become more efficient and more common and the cost per copy has come down.

In the late 1950s the major national library associations formed a joint committee to consider the problem of photocopying by libraries as fair use. The joint committee assembled information on the photocopying practices of libraries generally and conducted studies of the actual photocopying carried on in several large research and university libraries over a period of time. It concluded, in a report made in 1961, that what the libraries were doing in supplying to patrons upon request, single photocopies of copyright material, mostly of individual articles in journals, was in line with traditional library service and was not injuring copyright owners. It recommended that libraries adopt the policy of supplying a single photocopy of any material upon request, with the qualification that before making a copy of an entire work, the library should try to ascertain whether a copy is available through normal trade channels.

Many libraries have apparently been following, in practice, the principles enunciated in the gentlemen's agreement of 1935 or the policy recommended by the 1961 report of the joint committee.

Recently, two leading library associations have proposed to the Senate Subcommittee considering the copyright revison bill, that a provision be added to the bill absolving libraries from any liability for supplying a single photocopy of any work to anyone requesting it. Author and publisher groups have objected to an exemption of this breadth, and attempts to work out a special provision on library exemption acceptable to both sides have not succeeded. What the Congress may do on this issue, if anything, remains to be seen.

Meanwhile, these same groups have agreed that, in addition to the provision now in the bill permitting libraries to reproduce material in their manuscript collections for preservation or for deposit in other libraries, the bill should also provide for the making of single copies of published works in a library's collections to replace copies that are damaged or deteriorating, if unused replacements are not available for purchase.

V. PROSPECTS FOR THE FUTURE

It takes a bold and somewhat foolhardy prognosticator to venture any very clear prediction of what libraries will look like, and how they will supply material to the public, in 50 or even 20 years from now. Books as we know them will no doubt continue in use to some extent and for some purposes, but they will be supplemented and perhaps replaced in large measure by newer devices for recording, storing, reproducing, and transmitting the materials that make up libraries.

We are already familiar with processes of micro-reproduction that will give us all the pages of the usual book on a single card no larger than a present library catalog card, and we know of machines that will project magnified images from such microcards, page by page, for easy reading. Foreseeable is the further development of telephonic devices that will reproduce the printed page at any distant place connected with the telephone network, and of similar networks that will present images of printed matter on television screens whenever desired. In time, computers may be expected to contain in storage whole libraries of works that can be scanned and reproduced selectively upon demand wherever there is a hookup with the system.

There are some who envision the concentration of our whole body of intellectual resources in a few such systems serving large regions or the entire nation. If this should come to pass, many critical problems can be anticipated. Thus, selection will have to be made of the material offered for input into the systems. Who will operate the systems and make the selections? And will everyone have access to all the content of the systems? The dangers of censorship and the suppression of ideas may become greater than any we have yet had to face. Moreover, if works must be converted for input into a computerized system, how can their integrity be assured? And after their input, how can their integrity be maintained against the possibilities of manipulation and modification afforded by computer systems? The creators, disseminators, and custodians of our intellectual works, and the teachers and scholars who use them, will all need to concern themselves with questions of this nature.

Perhaps systems combining large-scale computer storage with network transmission facilities will operate as the major libraries of the future, and such systems may well merge the functions of processing, distribution, and reference service now performed separately by publishers and libraries, who will then become one.

Whatever may be the mechanisms for the performance of those functions in the future, it seems likely that copyright or something like it will persist as a means of stimulating the creation of new works, rewarding authors, and providing economic support for the mechanisms, old and new, by which works are processed and packaged for use and are distributed. Within the broad framework of these underlying purposes, the copyright law can be expected to undergo further major revisions to adapt it to the new technology and the new organization of functions, including the functions now performed by libraries. The study commission proposed in the pending legislation will have the monumental task of assessing what may be needed to keep the copyright law responsive to a hypothesized world of the future.

READING LIST

For a fairly comprehensive review of the copyright law in a relatively small volume, see: Howell, H. A., *Copyright Law,* rev. [4th] ed. (A. Latman), Bureau of National Affairs, Washington, D.C., 1962.

Ringer, B. A., and P. Gitlin, *Copyrights,* rev. ed., Practising Law Institute, New York, 1965.

For a summary discussion of the present U.S. copyright law and legislative proposals for its revision, see:

Report of the Register of Copyrights on the General Revision of the U. S. Copyright Law, House Committee on the Judiciary, Comm. Print, 1961.

Supplementary Report of the Register of Copyrights on the General Revision of the Copyright Law, House Committee on the Judiciary, Comm. Print, 1965.

House Report No. 83, 90th Cong., 1st Sess. on H.R. 2512 (1967).

ABE A. GOLDMAN

Copyright and the Public Interest

The quality of the culture of an age depends primarily on its intellectual and artistic creations. This quality is affected in turn by the appreciation, the protection, and the encouragement given their creators. The founders of our government recognized this basic public interest, and provided for it in the Constitution, reserving the power of protection to Congress rather than leaving it in the states. "The Congress shall have power . . . to promote the Progress of Science and useful Arts, by securing for limited Times to Authors . . . the exclusive Right to their respective Writings . . ." To encourage learning, to promote the arts, to preserve and develop our culture, the law gives the creator and the entrepreneur a right to control the use and disposition of their works in the form of copyright.

Literature, whether it be a scientific treatise or belles-lettres; art, whether it be a work of Matisse or an advertising poster; music, whether it be a symphony or the latest popular song, may all be copyrighted. The law of copyright is thus the law that help to shape the culture of our society, for it is a major factor in determining what books we read, what art we enjoy, what music we hear. Without the protection copyright gives to the creator and the entrepreneur, there would be little incentive to create and disseminate the works that constitute the repository of our learning and culture.

The price paid to the creator and the entrepreneur, however, is high, for copyright is a monopoly. The control of his work that the law gives to the copyright owner is absolute. He may or may not disseminate the work as he chooses; he may or may not make it available at reasonable prices and in sufficient quantities; and he may or may not let others copy the work, regardless of the motive of the copier or the lack of any impairment of the usefulness of the work to him.

The law of copyright is thus based on the profit motive, for the copyright owner is encouraged to make his work available only because to do so will bring him a monetary return. The successful functioning of the law of copyright to fulfill the public purpose of copyright, the advancement of learning, is made to depend upon whether the advancement of learning means a profit for the individual copyright owner.

This fact is unfortunate, not because profit is bad, but because the law delegates to the copyright owners a unilateral control of a large part of our culture. The law gives them rights, but exacts no correlative duties. In a society where freedom of expression is a paramount policy, the unrestrained power of an individual to suppress a given work, or even to control its use by others, by reason of his ownership of a copyright is manifestly inconsistent with the public interest.

Copyright is intellectual property, for its subject matter is creations of the mind. The property in the copyright is to be distinguished from the property in the copyrighted work, for in a legal sense property consists of nothing more than a series of rights the law will protect. A book, for example, has a physical form, but it is property only because the law recognizes in the owner the right to use and dispose of the book as he wishes. The copyright of the book has no physical form, but it is property because the law gives the owner of the copyright the right to control the disposition and use of the contents of the book. He may, for example, reproduce the book for sale, translate it, or dramatize it, which the owner of the book as a physical object may not do. It is this control over the use and contents of the book that constitutes the monopoly of copyright.

The problems that the monopoly of copyright poses have not gone unrecognized by the law. The Congress has limited the term of copyright. The courts have required strict compliance with the provisions of the copyright statute under pain of forfeiture of the work to the public domain; and they have created a doctrine of fair use, under which a person may make a reasonable use of a copyrighted work for limited purposes. Yet, these measures have not satisfactorily resolved the issue of monopoly. The term of copyright has been continually increased during our history; the forfeiture of a copyright often results in an injustice to the author or creator, as opposed to the publisher or entrepreneur; and the doctrine of fair use remains a nebulous one, the extent of which is unclear to all, even the courts.

The lawmakers have not satisfactorily resolved the problem of the monopoly of copyright because they have not developed a sound theory of copyright law. The reason for this failure, in turn, is that they treat copyright as protection for the author rather than as protection for the publisher, which in fact is its primary function. The essence of copyright is the right of exclusive publication. When a publisher publishes a work, copyright prevents a rival publisher from publishing that same work. The author, of course, is entitled to receive royalties from his publisher. But for the author to be entitled to receive royalties, it is not necessary that a publisher be entitled to publish a work exclusively. It is only more profitable for the publisher.

The fault of copyright law, then, is in treating copyright as an author's right rather than a publisher's right, and the error in characterization is a product of history rather than reason. It will be helpful to take a brief look at history.

The history of Anglo-American copyright is a long one, which begins in sixteenth century England under the Tudor monarchs. The story starts with the Stationers' Company, the London company to which all members of the booktrade—bookbinders, printers, and booksellers, i.e., publishers—belonged. The members of the company developed copyright to protect against the piracy by each other of published works. The stationer who first published a work had a right to continue exclusive publication of it. The stationers' copyright thus was a monopoly of a member of a company which was itself a monopoly.

The members of the company developed copyright for their own purposes, without any authorization or interference from the normal lawmaking agencies, the courts and Parliament. It is easy to see, then, why it was limited to members of the company, why it was deemed to exist in perpetuity, and why the author, who was not a member of the company, had no role in the development of that copyright.

The stationers were able to create and develop their own copyright because of the policy of government censorship in effect during the sixteenth and seventeenth centuries. The stationers' charter limited printing to members of the company to enable the government better to control the press, but the government was not interested in the private ownership of books and left the matter of copyright entirely to the company. When the last of the censorship acts, the Licensing Act of 1662, expired for the last time in 1694, the stationer's copyright was no longer protected by law.

The successor to the stationer's copyright was the statutory copyright, provided for by the Statute of Anne in 1710. The statutory copyright was based on and was similar to the stationer's copyright, with two major differences. It was not to exist in perpetuity, but was limited to a term of 14 years, with a like renewal term available to the author, "if then living"; and it was to be available to anyone, not merely members of the Stationers' Company.

The reason for these two changes was to destroy the monopoly of the booktrade which the perpetual stationers' copyright had enabled the publishers, or booksellers, as they were called, to build up and maintain. One concession the statute made to the booksellers, however, was to extend the old copyrights, the stationer's copyrights, the basis of their monopoly, for 21 years from the date of the act.

This provision of the statute enabled the booksellers to continue their monopoly unabated. Although the statute provided that anyone, including, of course, authors, could now obtain a copyright, the author could assign his copyright to the bookseller, and this is what the booksellers required as a condition for publishing a work. Thus, while the Statute of Anne enabled an author to obtain a copyright of his works, the statutory copyright was in fact no different in effect from the stationer's copyright, except that it was limited in time.

The statute did, however, provide a basis for the idea that copyright is an author's right, and when the old stationer's copyrights expired in 1731, the booksellers made use of this idea. Their purpose was to gain judicial recognition of a perpetual copyright despite the limitations provided in the Statute of Anne. The argument they presented to the courts was this: In addition to the statutory copyright, the author, because he created his work, has a perpetual common law copyright in that work. This copyright he could assign to the publisher, who, as an assignee of the author, would enjoy all the rights of the author.

The booksellers almost succeeded. The question, whether the author, as a creator of a work, had a perpetual common law copyright by virtue of his creation, was a live issue in England for some 40 years. The arguments the monopolists presented were best stated by Lord Mansfield, one of the great English judges, in the famous case of *Millar* v. *Taylor,* in 1769, which the booksellers won. If he does not retain the copyright after publication, said Lord Mansfield, "The author may not only be deprived of any profit, but lose the expense he has been at. He is no more master of the use of his own name. He has no control over the correctness of his own work. He cannot prevent additions. He cannot retract errors. He cannot amend; or cancel a faulty edition. And any one may print, pirate, and perpetuate the imperfections, to the disgrace and against the will of the author; may propagate sentiments under his name, which he disapproves, repents and is ashamed of. He can exercise no discretion as to the manner in which, or the persons by whom his work shall be published." Lord Mansfield's argument was summarized in the following statement. "His (an author's) name ought not to be used, against his will. It is an injury, by a faulty, ignorant and incorrect edition, to disgrace his work and mislead the reader."

These were powerful arguments. They state well the interest that an author has in controlling the use and disposition of his work, which can be summed up as an interest in maintaining the integrity of his work and the use of his name in connection with that work. There was only one thing wrong with Lord Mansfield's position. Copyright had never given the author these rights. As developed by the stationers, the scope of copyright protection had been limited to publishers. Moreover, to bring these rights of the author within the scope of copyright would serve only to enlarge the monopoly and would do little to aid the author, because almost certainly the practice of assigning the copyright to the publisher would be continued.

Lord Mansfield's enlarged concept of copyright as an author's right represented a victory for the monopolists. It gave them not only a perpetual copyright, it increased the measure of their control over copyrighted works. The victory was short lived. In 1774, in the landmark case of copyright law, *Donaldson* v. *Beckett,* the House of Lords overturned the decision in *Millar* v. *Taylor.* The *Donaldson* case accepted the premise that copyright is an author's right, and recognized that the author had a common law copyright in his works until they were published. But after they were published, the sole protection for the author was held to be the statutory copyright provided for by the Statute of Anne.

The reason for the decision was not any objection to the right of the author, but because of the booksellers' monopoly. The judges in the House of Lords perceived what Lord Mansfield did not state, that to recognize the author's common law copyright in perpetuity would be to continue the monopoly of the booksellers. Unfortunately, however, they did not perceive the fundamental change that Lord Mansfield's treatment of copyright as an author's right made in the concept of copyright, and they accepted his views on this point, at least implicitly.

The decision in *Donaldson* v. *Beckett* was important for this country. The first federal copyright act in 1790 was based on the Statute of Anne and when the Supreme Court interpreted that statute in *Wheaton* v. *Peters* in 1834, it naturally followed the *Donaldson* case, and the American copyright was the author's copyright first enunciated in the *Millar* case and limited by the *Donaldson* case.

The American lawmakers thus had from the beginning a fully developed concept of copyright. In one respect, this was fortunate, for it meant that the importance of copyright was early recognized in this country. In another respect, it was unfortunate, for the transfer of copyright as it developed in England to the new nation meant that the future development of copyright law was to be inhibited by historical precedent which, in many instances, was irrelevant for the United States.

The characterization of copyright as an author's right was the basis of the difficulty. This idea of copyright caused the lawmakers to view copyright as serving the interest of only two groups, the authors or creators and the user or purchaser of the copyright work. The primary function of copyright as protection for the publisher was obscured, and consequently the issue of copyright monopoly was concealed.

Had the lawmakers been aware from the beginning that law of copyright directly involved the interests of three, rather than two, groups, the issues would have been much clearer. The problem of monopoly would have been recognized as primarily a problem of the publisher and could have been dealt with directly. At the same time, a body of law for protecting the interests of the author apart from those of the publisher could have been developed. Moreover, it is probable that the treatment of all copyrighted works in the same way would not have occurred. There is a much greater difference between entrepreneurs of different kinds of works than between creators in terms of the rights which should be recognized. The music publisher, for example, has little in common with a book publisher, but the composer has much in common with the author. But the characterization of copyright as an author's right obscured the issues. Analysis of the problem was further hindered by the fact that the rights created by copyright were not acknowledged as belonging to either the author or to the publisher, but to the copyright owner.

The influence of historical precedent on copyright has resulted in a wholly unsatisfactory law of copyright, or at least this is the consensus of experts in the field.

As copyright law has developed in this country, for example, the monopoly of copyright has continually increased. The term of copyright in 1790 was a total of 28 years; today it is a total of 56 years; shortly, it will probably be the life of the author plus 50 years. The public interest has continually receded into the background as the copyright industry has become more and more profitable.

Manifestly, there is need to reconsider three of the basic ideas that have pervaded copyright law since the eighteenth century. The first is that the interest of the author or creator and the interest of the publisher or entrepreneur coincide so that they can be treated together under one copyright. The second idea is that all copyrighted works are entitled to be treated in the same way. The third is that the interest of the public is taken care of as an incident to copyright for the author and the publisher.

To start at the beginning, it is obvious that a satisfactory law of copyright requires a careful balancing of the interests of the members of three groups—the author or creator, the publisher or entrepreneur, and the user or the purchaser. The interests are interdependent, for the author must write in order for the publisher to publish and the user must purchase if the publisher is to publish.

The problem of balancing and reconciling these interests is essentially that of resolving the issue of control to eliminate the objectionable aspects of copyright as a monopoly. To what extent shall the power of controlling the use and disposition of a work be given to the creator, the entrepreneur, and the user?

The answer to this question depends upon control for what purpose, and the purpose depends upon the nature of the interest of each of the three groups. The creator wishes to control his work for two basic purposes. He wishes to protect the integrity of his work, as suggested by Lord Mansfield, because he has created it and the way in which it is exploited affects his reputation. He also wishes to profit from the use of his work.

The entrepreneur, on the other hand, has no claim to protecting the integrity of the work. His function is not to create, but to disseminate works, and his interest is a return on his investment. He wishes to control the work for purposes of profit.

The interest of the user coincides with the public interest, for it applies to all copyrighted works and to all persons. It is both an individual and a collective interest. The individual interest is to be able to make proper use of copyrighted works on reasonable terms for himself. The collective interest is that all other persons have the same right, for such a right is necessary to the development and dissemination of knowledge.

Once the interests of the three groups are identified, the ideas about copyright which are the obstacles to the development of a satisfactory law of copyright become apparent. They are two of the three ideas suggested above—the treatment of the interest of the author or creator and the publisher or entrepreneur under one copyright, that is the unitary treatment of the rights of the author and publisher; and the idea that all copyrighted works are to be treated in the same way, i.e., the unified treatment of copyrighted works.

As to the first idea, it is obvious that to enable the publisher of a work to profit from the publishing of the work, it is not necessary to give him the sole and exclusive right to publish that work for 56 years. Nor is it necessary to give him absolute control of the work to the exclusion of the author's control of his own creation. And as to the second idea, it is equally obvious that uniform protection for all works is neither necessary nor appropriate. A comic book does not involve the same interests as a scientific treatise, either for the author or for the public.

The approach to a satisfactory law of copyright, then, is to develop new copyrights based on two factors: (1) the identity of the owner of the copyright, whether it is to be the author or the publisher; (2) the nature of the copyrighed work and the extent of protection which is consonant with the public interest. If this approach is to be successful in eliminating the monopolistic aspects of copyright, the new copyrights must be limited in a way to make sure that a reasonable use of the work is a recognized right of the purchaser. And duties, as well as rights, of the copyright owner should be a part of the law of copyright. Thus, the nonavailability of a work could be grounds for a forfeiture of the copyright.

If there were an author's copyright and a publisher's copyright for the same work, the latter might be more limited in time than the former. The publisher, for example, might have the exclusive right to publish a work for 10 years, after which time others could publish it. But the expiration of the publisher's copyright would not necessarily mean the end of the author's copyright or the author's right to receive royalties from whoever did publish the work. At the same time, the law could provide that the user of the work has a right to use it in any way not inconsistent with the rights of the publisher or the author.

The suggested approach is not as radical as it may first appear, for it is already a part, a small part, of our copyright law in regard to music. The present copyright law provides that once a musical composition has been recorded, it may be recorded by anyone upon the payment of a license fee to the copyright owner.

This compulsory licensing provision, as it is called, is unique. It was enacted as a part of the law in 1909 in response to new technological developments and it was directed to the problem of potential monopoly in the recording industry. It has worked well. But the idea has not been utilized to solve problems of copyright in regard to other kinds of works. The reason, it seems, is that the recording of music was not subject to the inhibitions of historical precedent, as was the publishing of books.

The swift development of new forms of communication, which is the essential subject of copyright, has already made obsolete many ideas as to the law of copyright inherited from the past. Television, the computer, communication satellites, and electronic video tape recorders, to mention only a few developments, are not amenable to rules of law developed in the seventeenth and eighteenth centuries for the protection of books. These and other scientific developments will determine the shape of copyright law for the future, for the law must necessarily respond to needs. The response may be piecemeal, and thus almost certainly unsatisfactory; or it may be the result of foresight and wise planning to assure the use of new developments in the interest of the welfare of society. The latter course requires imagination and boldness and the discarding of the inhibitions of historical precedent.

LYMAN RAY PATTERSON

A Publisher's Viewpoint—Profit Seeking

The copyright law of the United States is based on Article I, Section 8, of the Constitution, which reads, "The Congress shall have Power . . . To promote the Progress of Science and useful Arts, by securing for limited Times to Authors and Inventors the exclusive Right to their respective Writings and Discoveries."

Two important observations can be made about this enabling Constitutional provision.

First, its basic purpose is to promote the public welfare, not to protect private interests, though the latter is implied as necessary for the former. (The implied basic right of an author to receive just compensation for his creative effort was firmly established at an early date by a landmark Supreme Court decision written by Justice Holmes.)

Second, it makes copyright a discretionary, rather than an absolute, Constitutional right—a fact that is often overlooked by authors, publishers, and other copyright proprietors. Thus, since the Congress has discretionary power to amend, or even to cancel completely, all law governing copyright protection, it is a mistake for copyright owners to assume that they are as permanently secure in ownership of literary works as in other rights that are absolutely secured to the individual under the Constitution—rights such as the ownership of real property, for example.

This difference has become increasingly apparent to authors and publishers in recent years—years which have seen demands for a sweeping revision of the current copyright law as codified in Title 17 of the United States Code. This law, enacted in 1909, has not had a thoroughgoing revision since its enactment. It is generally considered to be anachronistic and inadequate in many respects.

Another important observation about the basic nature of copyright under the U.S. law is that, although some have claimed it to be restrictive and monopolistic, it is actually extentional and propagative in function. Since copyright stimulates and rewards the creation, publication, and wide dissemination of original works of information, entertainment, and inspiration, it actually promotes rather than restricts the flow of knowledge for the material, intellectual, and cultural development of the nation. Since copyright protects only the "form of the embodiment" of ideas and information, it imposes absolutely no restriction on the flow and use of the ideas and information, or of the intellectual and cultural values, that are contained in copyrighted works. On the contrary, it seems obvious that without copyright the publication and dissemination of new works by creative writers, artists, scholars, researchers, and professional practitioners would be discouraged, and thus the flow of new ideas, new information, and learning itself would be seriously restricted.

It is important to note also that U.S. copyright law is based both on Title 17 of the U.S. Code and on a large body of case law established judicially by the courts. Since the basic statutory law is so outmoded, copyright owners in recent years have had to depend heavily on court law for protection of their interests. This dependence probably will continue indefinitely because several important areas of copyright regulation cannot be exactly and explicitly defined and fixed by legislation.

In order to register a claim to copyright, one has first to file an application on a prepared form available from the U.S. Copyright Office, The Library of Congress, Washington, D.C. When this application has been approved, the Register of Copyrights will issue a certificate of registration, with the requirement of a fee of $6.00 and a deposit of two copies of the registered work. Further, to qualify for registration, the work must contain a proper notice printed on the title page or the reverse thereof. The form of this notice must consist of the word "Copyright," or the symbol ©, accompanied by the name of the copyright proprietor and the year in which the copyright was secured. There are additional requirements for the registration of works by authors who are not citizens of the United States.

It should be noted that registration does not *guarantee* copyright protection; it merely establishes the author's claim and provides a basis for protection against possible infringement. For many published works, the copyright is registered in the publisher's name by permission of the author. This is done because the publisher usually is better equipped to protect the copyright and to deal in rights for reprint and translation of the work.

Under present U.S. law, the term of copyright is 28 years from the date of first publication. This term may be extended for another 28 years on proper application by the author or his heirs or assigns or executors. Application must be filed and the renewal registered within 1 year prior to the expiration of the original term. In recent years authors and other proprietors of copyright have advocated a change to a single term of copyright which would endure for the life of the author plus 50 years. Several arguments are advanced in favor of this change: (1) It provides better protection of the interests of an author who publishes successful works at an early age; (2) it avoids technical difficulties that are often encountered in the registration of renewals; (3) it conforms with the practice of most other major publishing countries of the world. The change is opposed by many public-interest spokesmen who think it would keep certain important works out of the public domain for unreasonably long periods.

The exclusive rights of the author in a copyrighted work are detailed in Section 1, Chapter 1, of Title 17. This section deals with rights to "print, reprint, publish, copy, and vend" the work; rights to translate or make another version; and rights to public delivery or performance and to recordings and transcriptions, with specified exemptions for certain uses of different classes of works. This section also deals, but quite inadequately, with the exemption of government publications. It gives no guidance on works produced under a government contract or grant.

Classes of works for which copyright may be claimed and registered are described in Section 5 of Chapter 1. Here the statutory statement is especially outdated and inadequate. It does not, of course, take into account the new technological processes for fixing, transmitting, and receiving (and thus "publishing") a work by electronic circuitry and electron-optical display. Neither does it give any guidance on the copyrightability of certain new kinds of works, such as computer programs and other "software" produced for computer-based informational and instructional systems.

Another important subject on which the present copyright law is widely considered to be inadequate is the practical matter of "fair use." For many years authors, publishers, and users of copyrighted works (and indeed many lawyers, as well) have been uncertain as to what is and what is not fair use of copyrighted material for such purposes as criticism, comment, news reporting, teaching, scholarship, and research. The present law is silent on the question of fair use, and through the years all efforts to enact a workable amendment covering this recognized limitation on the author's exclusive rights have failed. In this circumstance, a widely applied doctrine of fair use has evolved judicially through a large and wide-ranging body of case law, and still the question must be settled in each legally challenged instance by the courts. Many users of copyrighted materials, including educators, scholars, researchers, librarians, and operators of mechanized information systems, are unhappy with this situation, and often they have demanded explicit corrective legislation. On the other hand, many others who have practical and professional knowledge of the problem, including publishers, lawyers, and legislators, are convinced that fair use is susceptible neither to exact definition nor to explicit and workable legislation. They think that, as awkward and uncertain as the present practice may be, the present judicial determination must continue perforce.

In view of the described major shortcomings of the current copyright law (and many minor ones, besides), there has been in recent years, as noted earlier, a concerted effort to effect a thoroughgoing revision of Title 17 of the United States Code. This effort culminated in the introduction of revision bills in the 90th and 91st Sessions of Congress (in April 1967 and January 1969, respectively). In the planning and consideration of these bills, several critical issues have been developed and debated by opposing interests.

On one side, many educators, librarians, and information specialists have demanded explicit legislation for exemption of certain uses of copyrighted materials, including classroom teaching, scholarly inquiry, and scientific research. These demands have ranged all the way from a more liberal concept of fair use to a full right to use any copyrighted work in any way for "the public benefit." Some have gone so far as to want exemption of all not-for-profit uses of any kind. Others have argued that copyright should not be allowed to deter in any way the development of educational and informational systems employing the new technology for information transfer, or of extended use of educational and public-service television. All these demands are in terms of public welfare versus private interest. They have been exasperated by the increasing availability of high-speed, low-cost photocopying machines and other devices for quick and easy replication of copyrighted works. The crowning argument is that the present restrictions of copyright are not compatible with the modern technology of communications.

On the other side, authors, publishers, and corporate proprietors of copyrighted information have steadfastly opposed the public-interest efforts to erode copyright protection under the proposed revision of Title 17. They have argued not only in their own interest but also to the point that such erosion would in actual fact be against the public interest. They are convinced that the demanded exemptions, if granted, would destroy much of the present incentive for the creation of several important classes of books and much of their economic viability in publication.

Setting aside the moral question of equity under the law, copyright owners have stressed a simple practical point concerning incentives and economic viability. They contend that when it comes to authors' royalties and publishers' profit-and-loss statements, financial damage inflicted from nonprofit sources is no less hurtful than any other kind. Similarly, when it comes to already minimal markets for many specialized educational and professional books, erosion of these markets through copying for nonprofit uses is just as hurtful as any other kind of erosion. They are distressed to note the numbers of educators and scientists who have closed their eyes to these practical considerations. They have also noted the irony of the fact that many professional people are pressing for copyright exemptions which, if granted, would surely kill the very kind of publication that has to them the greatest professional importance.

No matter what course the efforts for revision may take, authors and publishers are likely to continue their insistence that a strong copyright law is the *sine qua non* of their economic existence, and that without such a law it will be impossible to publish many classes of works that are essential to the nation's welfare and security.

At the same time it seems apparent that many not-for-profit users of copyrighted materials will continue to insist that they must be given freer access to copyrighted works. Given this situation, most objective observers are counselling against hasty new legislation, particularly as it may affect the emerging confrontation between traditional protection and the as yet unknown requirements of the new communications technology.

CURTIS G. BENJAMIN

A Publisher's Viewpoint—Not-for-Profit

For nonprofit publishers the concern with copyright protection focuses on the impact of technological advances—specifically photocopying devices and the computer. These devices expand greatly the capacity to disseminate published information but create new problems as to how those who use the information are to contribute to support the publication function. Copyright protection is a major factor which enables the nonprofit publisher to fulfill his responsibility to make information available as widely as possible and still work out means for economic support of his publishing activity. This is consistent with the spirit of the copyright law which seeks to stimulate the production of literary and creative effort in the public interest rather than to provide economic guarantees to authors, publishers, or users.

It would be inconsistent with the goals and charter of nonprofit publishers to seek to restrict, forbid, curtail, or limit the use of material published under their copyrights. But no publisher, profit or nonprofit, can remain oblivious to the possible effects of photocopying or any other technology that might reduce the financial support available to continue the publishing function. To see that this economic support is not cut off is as much the responsibility of the user of published material as it is that of the publisher.

The position of nonprofit organizations on the matter of copyright protection can best be understood in terms of the whole spectrum of relationships that exist between professionals—scientists, teachers, doctors, lawyers, men of commerce—and the literature which they both create and use. Thus the nonprofit organization is, in effect, a group of professionals who provide financial support and give willingly and freely of their time as editors, authors, referees, and readers to maintain the information services of their profession. It is this same recognition of professional and social responsibility that guides the nonprofit organization in evaluating the impact of copyright protection on its ability to continue the publication of professional literature at a high level of quality and completeness as measured in terms of helping the professional make his contribution to the welfare of society.

The legal question is somewhat academic in connection with photocopying. The ultimate question of import to all concerned becomes, "Is photocopying a threat to the publishing function?" The data we have is at best sketchy in terms of confirming or denying the extent of any threat. It is known that copying is widely practiced and the number of copies made is large—very large. The report (*1*) of the Committee to Investigate Copyright Problems claims that "copying of published material amounted to at least 2 billion pages in 1967 and in 1969 will amount to 3 billion pages." Of this amount they estimate that 1.3 billion pages and 1.8 billion pages, respectively, are under copyright.

It is also worth noting that most of this copying is done under the assumption that there is no violation of the copyright law under the "fair use" concept when only single copies are made. Educators and librarians claim that the public interest requires a more liberal interpretation of the right to make copies while nonprofit publishers see a threat to continued publication in "fair use." But if the welfare and progress of our social-economic system is in any way dependent upon making available the results of research and technological development, then authors must be motivated to prepare such reports and in turn publishers must be encouraged to process those reports into forms that can readily be made available to all who have need for the information. The only possible definition of "fair use" is one that supports, not destroys, such a system.

Despite this volume of photocopying, nonprofit publishers would find it difficult to establish that photocopying has affected their ability to continue publication services. In his National Science Foundation study of 1962, Fry (*2*) stated that "if there is any area in which we might establish that photocopying has hurt subscriptions, it is in the case of library usage, particularly centralized research libraries which rely extensively on photocopying to fulfill loan requests." Fry added that such reliance was not yet heavy enough to cause significant damage as of that date. With the rapid increase in volume of photocopying, the situation may become more critical.

But the possible extent of such damage may well be significant since library subscriptions are important, particularly to journals of relatively low circulation. For example, a drop of 300 subscriptions to a journal selling for $30.00 a year could mean an increase of $3.00 in subscription price for a journal with about 3,000 subscribers. The effect would, of course, be more damaging for journals with fewer subscribers. One commercial publisher claims that the "burgeoning phenomenon of machine reproduction" has begun to force technical journals out of business (*3*). Thus it is clear that if photocopying is a threat to continued publication, some means must be developed whereby all who use published information make a fair contribution to the costs of publication, whether the financial arrangement be in the form of higher subscription prices, increased page charges to authors, or some form of payment for copying.

But of far more significance than any immediate threat to continued publication is the significance of copying—photo or otherwise—as a factor in the design of computer-based systems of disseminating and handling scientific information. To equate "fair use" concepts based on the traditional library concept and its limited clientele with a computer-based library system that has the potential of serving thousands of users is to take an unrealistic view of the economic requirements of the system from the viewpoints of both producers and users of scientific literature. Those who seek to have the input to computer-based systems admitted free of cost are either unaware of the economic consequences to publishers or they make a gross miscalculation of the way in which the data in computer-based systems will be available. The users of computer systems will, in the main, be the same users who can benefit from the use of existing sources of information. And, to the same extent, it is to be expected that they would share in the cost of operating the system. Just as a book is paid for at the time of being "put into the system," so a tape should be paid for at the time of input to a computer-based information system. In both cases the price must somehow be related to "sales" or use. Without recognition of the basic economic concepts involved, we bid for disaster and confusion in the dissemination and handling of scientific literature.

Nonprofit publishers, like their commercial colleagues, recognize that the pattern of future use is not yet well defined. Both are of the opinion that computer tapes of either the abstract type or whole copy must be protected in order to insure the growth of the machine system. The present controversy (4) represents a difference between those who wish to learn more about the patterns of future use before defining copyright protection versus those who fear the worst without being willing to put the matter to the test of time and use. During this trial period adequate protection must be insured for the author and the publisher. On this there can be no compromise.

We must recognize that in addition to new dimensions in terms of number of users and volume of literature we can make available to the user, automated systems will require new dimensions of cost. But we have yet to establish that the magnitude of the costs of processing and handling information by computer can be justified in terms of value to the research efforts of scientists. At the moment we operate on the basis of a high degree of expectation that the economic cost will be justified. In any event, it is quite likely that the cost of operating computer-based information systems will be relatively high with regard to the cost of processing the input to such systems and transmitting the information to the user. Thus the matter of input support may well become incidental to the much higher cost of operating information systems.

In an attempt to provide users with the broadest possible base for experimentation and development of information handling systems without concern for copyright restrictions, nonprofit publishers have launched several experimental programs designed to yield basic information on workable copyright arrangements. Included among these is the program of the American Chemical Society to provide its publications, including *Chemical Abstracts,* on microfilm under a licensing arrangement which permits the lessee to make photocopies from either the microfilm or print editions. Many nonprofit publishers are also entering into agreements to permit photocopying of their copyrighted material on a per-page-copied royalty basis.

In addition, many organizations are engaged in cooperative tests with users on the marketing of published information on magnetic tape. All of these programs should lead to an understanding of the kind of workable economic arrangements that can be developed between publisher and user in meeting the needs of computer-based systems of handling and disseminating information.

Clearly we are in a period of studying, testing, implementing, and evaluating major changes in the methods of disseminating and handling scientific and technical information. We speak of the obsolescence of the printed page and the cathode ray console as its replacement. The computer offers much in the way of promise but little in the way of achievement. Realization is going to take time, money, and a lot of dedicated effort on the part of both systems people and users of information. And until such time as we better understand the nature and operation of automated information systems, producers, publishers, and users have need to work toward developing a new level of understanding on how to deal with the copyright problems.

REFERENCES

1. Gerald J. Sophar and Laurence B. Heilprin, "The Determination of Legal Facts and Economic Guideposts with Respect to the Dissemination of Scientific and Educational Information As It Is Affected by Copyright," Washington, D.C., December 1967.

2. George Fry and Associates, "Survey of Copyrighted Material. Reproduction Practices in Scientific and Technical Fields," study completed March 1962, sponsored by National Science Foundation, George Fry and Associates, 135 S. La Salle St., Chicago.

3. "New Technology and the Law of Copyright: Reprography and Computer," *UCLA Law Rev.*, **15**(3), 943–944 (April 1968).

4. National Academy of Sciences, *Report on the Application of Copyright on Computer Usage,* December 1967, Washington, D.C.

J. H. KUNEY

The Viewpoint of the Librarian and Library User

For the American citizen the word "library" evokes far more meaning than just a collection of books. Our "free public libraries" and the vast majority of our institutional libraries, such as those of colleges and universities, are assemblies of books, selected, maintained, and kept accessible for highly altruistic purposes. As a people we are deeply committed to the apothegm "ye shall know the truth and the truth shall make you free."

Our libraries are public charities, established and maintained with both public and private funds. They are not primarily for the indigent, the poor, or the down-trodden: they are for rich and poor alike. They are established in the knowledge that only through cooperative effort can man begin to possess and control the vast flow of knowledge today. They are maintained in the belief that every citizen should have access to this knowledge and that the well-informed citizen is a better citizen.

THE USE OF LIBRARIES

Equally important is the conviction that many of those using the libraries are engaged in extending the boundaries of our knowledge.

This sense of serving both civic virtue and that highly altruistic and sometimes deeply utilitarian combination called "research" motivates society in supporting our libraries. No precise measures of the values produced by libraries has ever been found. Few, if any, would advocate or devise a general system for charging fees for the use of our libraries. The wide and random use made of our libraries both inspires collecting in the broadest dimensions and defies those who would seek to determine cost-benefits or set reasonable fees. It is virtually impossible to predict which of millions of volumes in a great research library will be used in a given day, week, or year. But each will have its time when no other of the millions will be a satisfactory substitute. Because of its basic philosophy, and because no other way of operation is feasible, the library is "nonprofit." The majority of its users are working for nonprofit purposes. Those who may ultimately derive profit are expected or required to compensate society in other ways.

The user of library books may be just a casual reader, or perhaps one who selects and commits to his own memory whatever he finds that he wants. He may be a student who takes notes as part of his learning process or who is preparing a "research paper" as a class assignment. The journalist, the literary critic, the historian, and others must borrow more heavily from previous writers in composing their works. The laboratory researcher may want to have at hand information on previous experiments as he performs his own work in extending the boundaries of knowledge.

As the information "explosion" continues, the indispensability of libraries grows proportionately greater and their operational problems increase. Libraries are the store houses, the organizers, and purveyors of past and present knowledge. Note-taking and copying is the incidental yet essential link to the new generation in its learning, and to the researcher or writer who is developing even more knowledge to put back into storage in the library.

In a very real sense, the function of the library is in close accord with the purpose of copyright as described in Article I, Section 8 of the U.S. Constitution: "To promote the Progress of Science and useful Arts."

Statute law and court decisions provide that the essential effect of copyright is to give the author or his agent the exclusive right to multiplication of copies for sale. Its basic purpose is to provide authors compensation for contributing to the common good by publishing their works. This compensation is something over and above the actual cost of manufacturing and distributing a book, but it is obtained only once, and no direct benefit accrues to an author (or publisher) from the resale of second-hand copies, for example. Copyright is not primarily for the benefit of the author but primarily for the benefit of the public.

A careful distinction must also be observed between the words as written and the ideas or thoughts expressed. In writing the copyright clause in the Constitution, our

Founding Fathers recognized that while a string of words may be tangible and possible to protect, the idea or thought is intangible and cannot be exclusive property. For the good of all, ideas, thoughts, and knowledge must be freely available and uncontrolled by any monopoly.

NATURE OF LIBRARY COPYING

Committing to memory is the most primitive and intangible form of copying. Manual copying whether by brush, pencil, quill, or ball point pen is as old as writing itself. Copying was once considered a virtuous activity. Saint Benedict endorsed it in his Rule. To this practice we owe the survival through the Dark Ages of many literary masterpieces of classical antiquity. The Bible itself has come down to us only through infinitely repeated copying. The great Gutenberg never heard of copyright. His development of printing was regarded primarily as an advance in the art of copying. His type was cut and cast to look like manuscript. The spread of the art of printing was duly opposed by the scribes, professional copyists, and amanuenses of the day.

The advent of the microfilm camera made copying easier and quicker, but less selective. The microfilm was handy, especially for copying archival materials for later review in the scholar's study. But the film gets the whole page, without any of the selectivity as to the more important or pertinent matter that manual note-taking or copying required.

The perfection of dry process, quick, automatic, coin-operated photocopy machines has been seen as a boon to the student or researcher who, in lieu of note-taking, gets copies of the important pages to be marked up and digested at leisure.

Numerous studies have been made to determine what harm, if any, this easy availability of photocopies has done to the copyright proprietor. To date no evidence has been produced to show any substantial damage in loss of sales to the proprietor. Actually a large proportion of the copies comes from works in the public domain, not subject to copyright.

Many proposals have been advanced to put meters on photocopy machines, to require stamps on photocopies, or to use other devices to collect and apportion royalties for library photocopying, but none has been regarded as workable. The fact that the authors' royalties and publishers' profits amount to only a fraction of a cent per page makes any equitable system of collection and distribution far more costly to operate than the amounts to be collected. No mere counting device on the copying machine would be fair because a substantial proportion if not a large majority of items copied are in the public domain. No way of control can be found for privately owned machines, or for publicly available ones in railway stations, drug stores, and countless other places.

Simple arithmetic tells us that single copying can never be anywhere near as cheap as multiple publication. This is still an age of mass production. No library copying machine can ever compete with the original product in quality, especially in illustrations.

In a sense the library is only the mechanism or middleman in the copying process. The test of infringement is the use to which the copied material is put. It is the library patron not the library which "uses" the copied material.

WHAT IS VALID COPYRIGHT?

The librarian, as well as the library patron, cannot be sure as to what actually is subject to copyright restriction and what is not.

The determination of what material may be actually subject to copyright is a very complex matter. The notice of claim customarily printed on the verso of a title page is only the first step. Unlike the Patent Office, the Copyright Office does not rule on the validity of copyrights. Anybody can print a notice or claim on almost anything. Except for prosecuting infringements or for certain other technical reasons, it is not even necessary to deposit a copy or file a form with the Copyright Office.

Casual browsing in new-book shelves, particularly among the paperbacks and reprints, will quickly turn up centuries-old classics in modern format with brand-new copyright claims.

A typical example is the well-known *Fanny Hill*. Although the story first appeared in print in 1749, a recent edition bears the copyright date of 1963. It has been said that the copyright date may cover the introductory material, but this introduction is almost wholly taken from contemporary reviews and comment of over two centuries ago. The classics of Malthus, Adam Smith, Isaac Newton, and a host of others can likewise be found covered with this presumptive mantle of protection, although it is obvious that copyright on these works long ago expired.

Some publishers have resorted to extended definitions of what they conceive copyright restrictions to be or what they would like us to think them to be. For example:

> All rights reserved. No part of this book may be reproduced or utilized in any form or by any means, electronic or mechanical, including photocopying, recording or by any information storage or retrieval system, without permission in writing from the Publisher.

This claim suggests the following questions: Why buy a book if you can't utilize it? What is the use if you are not allowed to read it and commit what you read to that most magnificent of all means of storing and retrieving information, the human brain?

Another notice apparently is intended to prevent libraries from putting a permanent binding on a paperback book:

> For copyright reasons this book may not be issued to the public on loan or otherwise except in its original soft cover.

This is indeed a weird extension of copyright—to prevent the binding of a book. Maybe the publisher thinks he has a patent on the book, bound or unbound. A patent gives its owner an exclusive right to a product or a process. He may use it himself; he may license others to use it, free or at a price; or he may prevent its use by anyone. Thus a patent controls the *substance* of a new development. A copyright is entirely different in this respect. It requires that the material be published—made available to the public generally.

The problem is more complex when a book goes out of print and is unobtainable. Then somebody may be willing to pay for a photocopy of the whole book. But if a publisher does not keep copies of his book available, how much right should he have to restrict others? Can he claim copyright if he won't make copies for sale?

Many librarians firmly believe that the privilege of copyright should carry with it the responsibility to make copies readily available. This principle operates in the music field, where there is compulsory licensing.

LIBRARY NETWORKS

Libraries, like other institutions, are undergoing change as our technology advances. To the extent that theirs is a distributive function, libraries are developing networks to interchange information about the location of books, and to make the books more broadly available through interlibrary loan. There is no evidence that libraries are buying fewer books and journals because of cooperation but rather that what they do buy are more broadly available. Certainly, the total library expenditure for books and journals has been rising rapidly in recent years.

Experiments in facsimile transmission to date have not proven technically satisfactory and certainly not economically feasible. The millennium when one copy of a book at the center of a facsimile transmission system will fill all library needs is far away indeed.

The analogy of community antenna (CATV) throws some light on the matter. CATV begins when people who can't get TV reception from the other side of the mountain or the tall office building get together to put up one high antenna and convey the signals to their homes by wire. On the theory that this device constitutes another broadcasting station of a sort, some proprietors, especially in music, have sought to collect a second series of royalties. In litigation carried to the U.S. Supreme Court, it was decided (1) that there was no legal claim for a second royalty on the theory that the Copyright Act does not give the copyright owner absolute control over every use of his works and that the CATV broadcast was not a "performance."

> Broadcasters perform. Viewers do not perform. Thus, while both broadcaster and viewer play crucial roles in the total television process, a line is drawn between them. One is treated as active performer; the other, as passive beneficiary.

> When CATV is considered in this framework, we conclude that it falls on the viewer's side of the line. Essentially, a CATV system no more than enhances the viewer's capacity to receive the broadcaster's signals; it provides a well-located antenna with an efficient connection to the viewer's television set. It is true that a CATV system plays an "active" role in making reception possible in a given area, but so do ordinary television sets and antennas. CATV equipment is powerful and sophisticated, but the basic function the equipment serves is little different from that served by the equipment generally furnished by a television viewer. If an individual erected an antenna on a hill, strung a cable to his house, and installed the necessary amplifying equipment, he would not be "performing" the programs he received on his television set. The result would be

no different if several people combined to erect a cooperative antenna for the same purpose. The only difference in the case of CATV is that the antenna system is erected and owned not by its users, but by an entrepreneur.

In a sense, this affirms the long assumed right that once a library bought a book, it could lend it or display it in any way it chose. The reader might look at the book with magnifying glasses, microscopes, mirrors, or by television.

FAIR USE

Because the statute law is silent on library copying, a doctrine of "fair use" has been developed partly through court decisions, partly through actual practice, and partly through cooperative efforts between librarians and publishers.

The very purpose for which statutory copyright is granted requires that the public be permitted to make any and all uses of the copyright material, except for the limited monopoly granted to the author for a limited time to publish and sell. This leads to the question of what is fair use and what is unfair, or infringement. Fair use is not, as it has been termed by some, a form of infringement which is condoned. The use of copyrighted material in all ways that do not interfere with the limited monopoly granted to the author is inherent in the copyright law and constitutes the justification for statutory copyright. Historically and basically, copyright may be considered from a practical point of view as the right to sell multiple copies and to profit thereby.

The difference between infringement and fair use is a matter of purpose, degree, and the effect of the copying rather than the act of copying or publishing as such. The differentiation between fair use and infringement is fundamentally a problem of balancing what the author must dedicate to society in return for his statutory copyright (which varies according to the nature of the works involved) against undue appropriation of what society has promised the author in terms of protection of his exclusive right to make merchandise of the product of his intellectual work.

The meaning of "copy" in copyright is actually related to multiplication of copies and publishing for sale, and the courts have frequently ruled that copyright does not restrict the scholar from taking notes for individual and private use. Of course, as a matter of practicality, it would be impossible to prevent such note-taking, even if it were illegal.

The ultimate extension of this principle of fair use is found in the rights of reviewers and others to quote and republish in unlimited multiple copies extracts from copyrighted works.

Parenthetically it may be observed that to a considerable extent photocopying is done of learned journal articles. In writing these the author gets little or no compensation. Often he must subsidize the publication. As soon as possible he sends out reprints. His objective is to get as wide an exposure as possible. Library photocopying is just one more path toward this objective.

The problem of photocopying in libraries has long been the subject of study and discussion. The development of photostat service in large reference libraries in the

1920s first aroused the concern of book publishers. An attempt to clarify the situation was made in the thirties with the concluding of a gentlemen's agreement between the Joint Committee of Materials for Research and the National Association of Book Publishers, the trade association of book publishers which has since gone out of existence.

Although the agreement was later made the basis of a Material Reproduction Code, prepared by the Association of Research Libraries and adopted in 1940 by the American Library Association, it did not really clear the air.

As the outgrowth of further discussion, the Joint Libraries Committee on Fair Use in Photocopying was constituted in 1957. An extensive report was presented in the ALA Bulletin for June 1961 (Vol. 55, pp. 571–573). A summary statement was distributed to the ALA Council as part of the ALA Copyright Issue Committee report in January 1964. Its findings were as follows:

> 1. The making of a single copy by a library is a direct and natural extension of traditional library service.
> 2. Such service, employing modern copying methods, has become essential.
> 3. The present demand can be satisfied without inflicting measurable damage on publishers and copyright owners.
> 4. Improved copying processes will not materially affect the demand for single-copy library duplication for research purposes.

THE REVISION MOVEMENT

Recognizing the need for classification and some revision in the copyright laws, the Register of Copyrights in the Library of Congress sponsored a series of thirty-four studies of various aspects of the laws, and proposed revisions. These are reviewed and summarized with recommendations by the Register of Copyrights in *Copyright Law Revision,* 1961, 87th Cong. 1st sess., House Committee Print.

Diverse groups were organized to develop respective points of view and protect their interests. Book publishers, textbook publishers, music publishers, juke-box operators, book manufacturers, printers unions, educators, and librarians all have participated in discussions with the register and hearings before congressional committees. Powerful lobbying, particularly relating to the CATV issue, by the groups with big money at stake, especially the music composers and publishers, the broadcasters, and juke box operators, has helped prevent enactment of revision bills.

The American Library Association established a Committee on Copyright Issues to study revisions and make recommendations. This committee succeeded in alerting librarians to the threat of loss of photocopying rights, and as guidelines for presentations to various groups, for the information of the Register of Copyrights, for testimony at House and Senate committee hearings, and as basic policy for all to know, the committee presented the following eight resolutions to the ALA Council. Numbers 1–6 were approved at Chicago in January 1964 and 7 and 8 at Saint Louis in July 1964.

1. That the principle of "fair use" be reaffirmed.
2. That the requirement of printing of notice and date of copyright be endorsed as absolutely essential to libraries and library users.
3. That proposals to make the duration of copyrights be for a fixed term, both for published and unpublished works, be endorsed.
4. That the principle that libraries be exempted from import restrictions and penalties be reaffirmed.
5. That the principle that government material should not be subject to copyright be reaffirmed.
6. That proposals to have copyright subsist in the Federal Government after its expiration in the hands of the copyright owner be opposed.
7. That the requirement of American manufacture as a qualification for securing copyright of works by American authors be opposed.
8. That the "not for profit" principle as now embodied in the copyright law be endorsed.

Discussion of copyright revision has produced a spate of suggestions and a number of bills introduced in Congress which adversely affect library interests. Among the threats was one which amounted to a proposed tax on library book purchases to be used to support museums and the performing arts, with the ultimate result of benefiting music publishers by reducing competition from uncopyrighted music used by radio and TV broadcasters (2).

One member of a self-appointed committee of copyright lawyers has boasted that they have developed restrictions on every means of transmission of thought except smell, taste, and extrasensory perception. The basic trouble with this committee, from the librarian's point of view, is that it is made up of men who are devoted to helping their clients look for more money or special privilege in copyright. Nobody is giving much thought to the consumer. Nobody is thinking in terms of librarians who seek only to serve and who do not see any additional sources of income for themselves in any exploitation of copyright or in the use of copyrighted material.

Numerous proposals have been advanced to set up clearing houses to monitor photocopying in libraries and collect royalties therefor. But even the publishers admit nothing practical has evolved so far.

Publishers in the United States have agreed that they do not now seek the "lending right" which obtains in Scandinavian countries and which has been advocated in Britain. This provides an extra financial return to authors and publishers on books bought and lent by public libraries.

The ultimate in the philosophy of license for use is stated in terms of modern technology by Laurence Heilprin, who writes, "A copyrighted work is essentially a message. A copyright is a legal privilege to attempt to control part of a communication system. . . . It is the right to derive economic benefit from the market value of a message"(3).

DURATION OF COPYRIGHT TERM

The problem of how long copyright should last is a vexing one. The present term is 28 years, subject to renewal for 28 years. According to statistics compiled by the

Copyright Office, only 15% are renewed after the initial 28 years. There is strong sentiment among authors and publishers to have the term extended to 50 years after the death of an author, considerably longer than present practice.

Libraries, who are the principal buyers of old books, would bear the great proportion of the burden of this extension. Conversely, the reprinting of out-of-print items would be much handicapped. It does not seem fair to have copyright remain so long after the poor paper on which the text is printed has turned to dust.

For hundreds of more or less obscure authors whose deaths are relatively unnoticed by the biographical reference tools, the problem of fixing the date (50 years later) of the expiring of their copyright would be practically insolvable. Certainly the proposed change could often involve far more work and far greater uncertainty than the arithmetic of copyright notice date plus a specific number of years.

For unpublished manuscripts the copyright is presently, under common law, perpetual—or until the manuscript is printed and published. Current proposals would impose a term upon manuscripts, a welcome relief to librarians, archivists, and scholars.

SUMMARY AND BIBLIOGRAPHY

On balance it would seem that librarians and library patrons have very little to gain and much to lose in copyright revision. They find themselves pitted against proprietors seeking to restrict or abolish the time honored "fair use" and "not for profit" principles; and proposing blanket restraints on display of material through television screens, computers, and facsimile transmission.

In the long run the big issues will be decided in big money terms, typical of the battle between music composers and publishers versus juke-box operators and CATV.

The history of copyright revision is contained in a score or more of reports issued by the Copyright Office, in reports of congressional hearings, and in various law journals. A comprehensive summary is the Report of the House Committee on the Judiciary of 1966 (89th Cong. 2nd sess. Report No. 2237). Unfortunately, it does not appear that library and library user interests are fully represented, especially in such phrases as (p. 64), "where the unauthorized copying displaced what realistically might have been a sale, no matter how minor the amount of money involved the interests of the copyright owner need protection."

The present writer has issued fuller and more detailed statements at various hearings, and summarized them in "The Copyright Grab Bag I, II" in *ALA Bull.*, **60**, 46–55 (January 1966), and **61**, 707–712 (June 1967).

Professor Julius Marke, Law Librarian of New York University has written *Copyright and Intellectual Property,* Fund for Advancement of Education, 1967. He gives special attention to the problems of copyright on government financed materials.

Verner W. Clapp, formerly Deputy Librarian of Congress and recently retired president of the Council on Library Resources, has written an intriguing and compelling history of copyright: *Copyright: A Librarian's View,* Association of Research Libraries, Washington, D.C., 1968.

Another librarian, Ralph Shaw, formerly Director of the Rutgers Library School, has issued a strong and forthright challenge on behalf of library practices: *Literary Property in the United States,* Scarecrow Press, Washington, D.C., 1950.

A calm and literal view of the whole situation is that of Prof. Benjamin Kaplan of Harvard Law School: *An Unhurried View of Copyright,* Columbia Univ. Press, New York, 1967.

M. B. Schnapper, Editor, Public Affairs Press, Washington, D.C., inveighs against copyright for private profit of government publications, government sponsored research reports, and of speeches and reports by government officials in *Constraint by Copyright,* Public Affairs Press, 1960. He also accuses some government agencies of seeking to use copyright as a means of restriction or suppression of information.

In 1968 the Williams & Wilkins Co. of Baltimore, Maryland, publishers of numerous medical and scientific journals, filed in the U.S. Court of Claims a claim against the National Medical Library for damages because of photocopying of certain periodical articles by the library. This case is expected to become an important milestone in the history of library photocopying. An *Amicus Curiae* brief, prepared by Cox, Langford & Brown, of Washington, D.C., has been filed jointly by the Association of Research Libraries, the Medical Library Association, and the American Association of Law Libraries. This brief is an excellent statement in support of the contention that "the exclusive right to 'copy' claimed in the present case is not provided for in the Copyright Act," and that even if it were held that there was such an "exclusive right," the "particular use of copyrighted material in this case would not provide a basis for an action for infringement." Adjudication of this case is not expected until 1972 and there may be appeals. Docket No. 73–68.

REFERENCES

1. *Fortnightly Corp.* v. *United Artists, Inc.,* 392 U.S. 390, 20 L. Ed. 2d, 1176, 88 S. Ct. 2084 (1968). Reh. Den. 393 U.S. 902, 21 L. Ed. 2d, 190, 89 S. Ct. 65 (1968).

2. Eighty-seventh Congress, 2nd sess., H.R. 9906. A bill to provide for the establishment of a national arts agency by Representative Harris B. McDowell, Jr. (D., Del.). See also remarks by Mr. McDowell in *Congressional Record* (House, 1962), pp. 17227–17229.

3. Laurence B. Heilprin, "Technology and the Future of the Copyright Principle," *Phi Delta Kappan,* **48**(5), 220–225 (January 1967).

CHARLES F. GOSNELL

The Viewpoint of the Computer Scientist

In his monumental treatise on copyright (1), Nimmer quotes an opinion of the Court of Appeals which begins: "This action for copyright infringement presents us with a picture all too familiar in copyright litigation: a legal problem vexing in its difficulty, a dearth of squarely applicable precedents, a business setting so common that the dearth of precedents seems inexplicable, and an almost complete absence of guidance from the terms of the Copyright Act (2).

Few observers would quarrel with Nimmer's conclusion that this represents a "generally accurate appraisal of the present status of copyright law," an "area of the law which is almost, if not entirely, unique . . . [since] copyright represents an application of one of the oldest branches of law, property, to one of the more striking recent developments of our contemporary culture, the phenomenon of mass communications" (1).

It may be helpful to consider that copyright is an attempt to reconcile three distinct interests in an intangible. First of all, there is the originator, the person who creates the expression; in the constitutional sense, the *author*: "He to whom anything owes its origin; originator, maker" (3).

The second distinctive interest is that of the *publisher*. This entity takes that which has been created by the author and transmits it to the recipient. "The role of the publisher in the realm of intellectual property is substantially different than that of the author. . . . The function of the publisher is almost exclusively entrepreneurial: he contracts with an author for the right to issue a book, then contracts with others to have the book printed and bound, and finally contracts with bookstores or book-clubs to have the book sold to the reading public " (4).

The third, but by no means least of the identifiable interests, is that of the *users*, who buy, read, and make use of the creation; in McLuhan's phrase, "the percussed victims of the new technology" (5).

All three of these interests coalesce in their pursuit and exploitation of that entity which is the object and result of the authorship, publishership, usership, and surely copyrightship, the so-called "writing" which is the "matter and form of a literary or artistic work" (6).

All four of these copyright terms—author, publisher, user, and writing—are sufficiently imprecise and lacking in epistemological or legal certitude as to be a valid means of communicating the tensions and problems which afflict the computer scientist. In the McLuhan sense, he has become the media by which what were four distinct compartments have become an amorphous whole. In an existential sense, he *is* the author, publisher, user, and, in many instances, the writing as well.

Notwithstanding, it is useful to examine how copyright affects him professionally as well as culturally.

COPYRIGHTED MATERIAL AS DATA

The computer scientist, particularly if he is working in the information retrieval field, is concerned with the materials that he may use in his systems. In a sense he is a lazy creature. If he wishes to use some literary material as a corpus and he finds that such use is prohibited or bordered with barbed-wire restrictions, he may abandon his line of inquiry or utilize some less meaningful source of material. It seems clear that the present and foreseeable technology will not replace the printed text as the primary means of transmitting intelligence in the mass (7), except to a most limited degree (8). On the other hand, he, and, more importantly, his sponsoring organization, do not wish to expend their limited research funds in quixotic legal battles, particularly when they are placed on notice that the publisher is prepared to battle on "principle" (9).

Hence, it may be useful to examine certain areas where the computer scientist is utilizing copyrighted literary data as a corpus for his manipulations.

These areas may be further divided into the relative quantity of the original material utilized in his computer system.

Whole Text Input

At present there are only a few areas where the computer scientist needs the complete text as input. Some spectacular experiments have been the establishment of authorship of particular essays of the Federalist Papers (10), consistency between the *Iliad* and the *Odyssey,* and single authorship of books of the Bible (11). Less spectacular but apparently equally useful are the creation of concordances and other bibliographic tools for the humanistic researcher.

As one scholar has noted, "The computer is taking over jobs which represent dog work for the scholar; the computer can do such tasks more rapidly, more efficiently, and more effectively than can the scholar" (12).

At the present time, and for the foreseeable future, full text input is costly in preparation and costly in storage availability. While some publishers have made the paper tapes, which represent their text, available, even these must be converted to computer adaptable language at significant cost. Despite significant advances in memory size and reductions in costs of storage per bit, machine stored full text is still prohibitively expensive for all but research purposes. Notwithstanding the aforementioned costs, there is a significant body of literature available for experimentation. Here, however, the researchers are taking great pains to publicize the availability of the works in full text so as to avoid unnecessary duplication (13).

Another area of research has been that of the inquirer/questioner. Here a general type of reference work, such as a dictionary or an encyclopedia, is put into the system as a fact base for later inquiry and/or manipulation.

As will be seen, this latter use of complete material has greatly frightened the traditional publisher of technical reference works.

Full text input has also been of importance in conjunction with research on mechanical translation. While the earlier optimism regarding the possibility of fully automatic translation no longer prevails (14), much effort is continuing in syntactic and semantic analysis. Here again large bodies of complete text are necessary to validate tentative results. The computer scientist here is developing generalized methods of preparing concordances, particularly where the syntactic environment of the word is the center of interest (15).

Still another area that is dependent upon access by computer to the whole text is automatic indexing, and possibly abstracting; i.e., "the use of machines to extract or assign index terms [or prepare abstracts of the underlying material] without human intervention once programs or procedural rules have been established" (16).

After an initial surge of interest, it too, like mechanical translation (14), has run into significant difficulties in translating prophecy into practice where theoretical insights are still to be developed.

Other areas of research which utilize full text seem free of copyright considerations since they utilize materials that are clearly in the public domain. Thus full text input of laws and legal cases into an information retrieval system would pose no significant copyright problems (17).

One of the major battles raging about the current efforts to revise the Copyright Laws is the concern as to whether entry into an automated computer system is to be controlled by the author or publisher (27).

At one extreme, the Register of Copyrights has stated:

> It seems clear, for example, that the actual copying of entire works (or substantial portions of them) for "input" or storage in a computer would constitute a "reproduction" under clause (1), whatever form the "copies" take: punchcards, punched or magnetic tape, electronic storage units, etc. Similarly, at the "output" end of the process, the "retrieval" or "print-out" of an entire work (or a substantial part of it) in tangible copies would also come under copyright control (28).

As one proponent of the most restrictive controls over the use of copyrighted works as input observed:

> Kaminstein's forthright opinion that the mere input of a copyrighted work into a computerized system would clearly be an infringement under the new law came as a surprise, not to say a shock, to many people. They could not agree that storage could be considered as copying, or even as the making of a "derivative" work. Nor did they understand that the possession of a copy of a work does not give the owner any property rights whatever in the work itself—that the purchaser of a book has indeed bought no more than the right of access to a certain literary or scientific work through the physical form of the particular copy purchased (29).

Partial Text Input

Copyright considerations alone may dictate that the computer scientist only utilize portions of text in his retrieval input. Thus many courts which would question the copying of an entire or major portion of a work for input (18), even for scholarly, educational, or research purposes (19), might not look with disfavor upon the use of portions or fractions of books.

Of particular interest is the widespread use of KWIC (Key-Word-in-Context) indices. Here ready acceptance has flowed from the speed with which a complete index to some specific set of reference materials can be produced:

The KWIC type process is indeed simple and straightforward. The words of the author's title are prepared for input to the computer by keystroking, either to punched cards or to punched paper tape. After being read by the computer, the text of a title is normally processed against a "stop list" to eliminate from further processing the more common words, such as "the," "and," prepositions, and the like, and words so general as to be insignificant for indexing purposes, such as "demonstration," "typical," "measurements," "steps," and the like. The remaining presumably "significant" or "key" words are then, in effect, taken one at a time to an indexing position or window, where they are sorted in alphabetical order. The result is a listing of each such word together with its surrounding context, out to the limit of the line or lines permitted in a given format. As each keyword is processed, the title itself is moved over so that the next keyword occupies the indexing position, and this process is repeated until the entire title has thus been cyclically permuted.

A number of formats are available in which the length of the line, the position of the indexing window, and the extent of "wrap-around" (bringing the end of a title in at the beginning of a line to fill space that would otherwise be left blank) are major variables (20).

Little problem would arise from copyright considerations in copying titles since, "for the most part, copyright may not be claimed in a title" (21). However, the copying of lists of titles, which lists themselves are properly the subject of copyright, would be a form of full-text input, and would be subject to "fair use" exemptions and restrictions.

In this connection, it is noteworthy that due to the economic problems alluded to earlier, some experiments which started off in full text for a data corpus have since gone to already available abstracts and synopses. Thus the LITE system (22), which began with full text input of federal and state statutes, has confined itself to manual terms selected by human indexers for an important area of decisional law input (23).

At least one authority has indicated that, despite the broad freedom of unauthorized use commonly accorded legal materials (17), copyright restrictions will apply to a meaningful human abstract of the same materials, i.e., even though the full text may be utilized, the headnote or digest may not (24).

Whole Text Output

As has been noted (7), at present there is little commercial incentive to output the complete text of a work of significant length. Even with the highest speed printers, and allowing for a considerable drop in peripheral costs, which seems unlikely, it is doubtful that a computer can replace the printing press, where the entire text has been stored or transferred through the memory. In the absence of significant economic erosion, the courts have been most reluctant to prohibit noncompetitive uses of copyrighted materials, even in full text (25).

The few examples to the contrary may be distinguished on the peculiar fact situations presented (26), or perhaps even by the eminence of counsel representing the plaintiff on appeal (19). Notwithstanding the present state of the law, which would seem to exempt even the full text output of copyrighted materials until such time as such becomes the actual rather than the hypothetical threat to the original proprietor, changes may be in store.

Partial Text Output

Here there is a more difficult area, since it may already be commercially feasible to produce limited output and even destroy an existing market.

Benjamin gives us a vivid example:

> Nor could one usually argue that a computer print-out of a few figures or formulas or of small selections of data would contravene the "fair use" doctrine as it has been established by the courts.
>
> Yet the foregoing are exactly the kinds of use that are customarily made of handbooks, data books, and other basic reference works in science and technology.
>
> Let us suppose that a large corporation—say a Monsanto or a Du Pont—has established a company-wide (and hence a nationwide) computerized technical information system for use at the touch of dozens of consoles by its hundreds of scientists and engineers. Let us also suppose that the "hardware" camp has prevailed in the copyright argument and that the corporation is free to store the whole of Perry's *Chemical Engineers' Handbook* in its computerized system. Let us finally suppose that the corporation buys one copy of this handbook, stores its content, and then puts it to the seemingly "fair" uses described above. Obviously, in a situation such as this the one stored copy could take the place of as many as 500 or even 1000 copies of the handbook as it is now used. And if eight or ten other large corporations did likewise, there would be no remaining market sufficient to sustain publication (*29*).

Hence, it is not entirely impossible that a court could reasonably find that, due to the state of technology—cost of memory for storage, etc.—whole text output would not be unreasonable whereas partial output would constitute infringement. The test would be the relative measure of the competing copies. To use Benjamin's example, if it costs $2,000 to output the complete Perry's *Chemical Engineers' Handbook* whereas a single copy may be purchased from McGraw-Hill for one tenth that, a court might well allow such full text output. However, if a company were to purchase one copy and use it as described to avoid the purchase of additional hard copies, then such use might well be held illicit today.

No Output

Here there seems few problems of copyright significance to the information retrieval scientist. At present there are no restrictions on the use of books from the library shelf as a reference source in solving problems or compiling data.

Similarly, once the copyrighted work has been fully stored in a computer system, its mere use or manipulation for analysis or problem solving would not be unfair. Thus, the preparation of a concordance or a word frequency analysis would be unexceptional (*12*).

Conclusions

Heretofore the discussion has centered around the types of *textual* material utilized for information retrieval and computer usage. Of necessity, reference was limited to printed matter, generally in book or periodical format. The conclusion reached was that due to the enormous expense presently incurred in converting textual material to machine readable format, and vice versa, it is unlikely that copyright considerations will interfere with experimental use. To be specific, as of this writing, optical readers are reasonably able to handle only an unaesthetic uppercase-and-numerics-only font (30). The technology necessary to allow automatic reading of multifont straight textual material can be described as being in an early experimental stage at best. Bluntly put, there have been no significant breakthroughs in the mechanics of putting nonmachine data into a computer and obtaining the results. While memory sizes have increased exponentially, and memory speeds have gone from multiseconds to nanoseconds, and costs of memory have dropped by orders of magnitude per storage bit, the devices which put data in and out have remained relatively static in costs, speeds, and capacities (31).

Based upon these considerations, it is suggested that for the present most copyrighted materials may be introduced into information retrieval and storage systems, if the text is converted into machine language. However, if the owner of the copyright or each piece of material used by the system must be contacted prior to input for permission to use the material, then research in this area becomes difficult if not impossible.

While most copyright proprietors seem to be willing to grant permission to use copyrighted material, some may not. However, the necessity for writing to secure permission may be enough to lead researchers, who are not lawyers and may not wish to be put to the trouble of securing permissions well in advance of their experiments, to spend their time in other ways. Avoidance of copyrighted material may have an unfortunate inhibiting effect upon research in the area of automatic information storage and retrieval, and would perhaps completely bias any experimental results.

In another area, many abstracts to be used in information retrieval systems are copyrighted. Writing to secure permission, if such were held necessary, from thousands of individual owners of copyrights on the abstracts as well as on the original material could prove sufficiently burdensome to the designers of the information systems to discourage them from including copyrighted material in their systems. It may be difficult if not impossible, for example, to secure permission to use abstracts of old or out-of-print articles from the author, the publisher, and the abstractor. A different question is raised when the copyrighted material is not converted to machine language for relay *through* a computer. Instead, the computer is used to locate the document and assist in its handling (32). Here traditional copyright doctrine would apply and the special considerations alluded to above would not be expected to apply.

The Problem of Making Copyright "Input" an Infringement (33)

Arguments in Favor of Making "Input" an Infringement. There are several arguments in favor of making computer input an operation requiring compensation. First, copyrighted material may be fed into a computer and emerge later not in the form of a reproduction, but rather in the form of useful information—such as an answer to a question. When output takes this form it is possible that no compensation might be due at the "output" stage. And, if there is widespread use of the copyrighted material contained within the computer in this way, the sale of the books and journals that the computer contains may decline. For this reason, it is claimed, compensation should be paid, and it must be paid, at the point of input or otherwise it might not be paid at all.

Second, the publishers have argued that unless compensation is exacted at the "input" stage, they may not be able to obtain any compensation for material that is rarely used. For example, at the present time a publisher may sell a copy of a scientific work to each of 10,000 libraries. If these libraries are connected with a computerized information system, however, he may sell only one copy to the system owner. While he will be able to collect royalties whenever the book stored within the computer is called for by a subscribing library (for a reproduction printed on paper or projected on a screen will then be made), it is conceivable that the book may be called for less than 10,000 times a year.

Third, the publishers argue that unless a toll is exacted at the computer input stage, they will have difficulty discovering violations of their copyrights. It is difficult to see why this is so, for, although it may be difficult to keep track of the number of reproductions that the computer makes of a copyrighted work, it is as easy to discover that a computer has made at least one reproduction as it is to discover that a copyrighted work has been fed into the computer in the first place. In fact, one method of showing that work had been put into a system without authorization might be to show that a reproduction had come out of the system. A fee schedule could easily be arranged which simply makes a part of the royalty charge for the first reproduction coming out of the machine that amount that might otherwise be charged as a royalty for input.

Finally, the publishers argue that unless compensation is required at the input stage, they will not be able to make money from selling "machine readable" copies of their books or journals. This argument seems to be another form of the first argument just discussed. Publishers will be able to make money from selling or leasing machine readable copies of their books or journals. It is true, however, as we have just stated, that a copyright toll will not be charged if the copyrighted material emerges not as a reproduction but in the form of an answer to a question. And, insofar as this type of activity replaces the sale of books or journals, publishers and authors may be injured.

Arguments Against Making "Input" an Infringement. Several arguments can be advanced against assessing a copyrighted toll at the "input" stage. First, at the present time almost all copyrighted material fed into a system will emerge in the form of a reproduction. With the possible exception of mathematical tables, certain types of compilations, and similar scientific material, computers by and large do not store and use the full text of copyrighted material to answer questions directly, nor is there reason to believe that they will be able to do so in a significant way in the immediate future. The problem that the situation presents should not be resolved now, but we can wait until we see what actually happens.

Second, insofar as computers can operate directly upon copyrighted material stored within them to solve problems, etc., such operations do not necessarily replace the sales of books or journals. They may stimulate such sales. To impose a copyright toll may discourage the use of such material in computers or retard the development of this type of computer use. There is no reason to pay authors a fee (and at the same time inhibit the use of computers) when no interference with the sale of copyrighted material can be shown.

Third, since almost all copyrighted material now going into computers emerges in the form of a reproduction, and since a toll is thus imposed at the "output" stage, to impose a toll at the input stage is, at the present time, redundant. (Since the *amount* of the toll results from bargaining between users and copyright holders, it should not be affected significantly by the fact that a user is bargaining for the right to reproduce at the output stage rather than for rights to both input and output.)

Fourth, certain users of copyrighted material are exempt from the copyright toll. For example, S. 597 (the Copyright Revision Bill) provides that no royalty need be paid when material is used as part of "face-to-face" teaching. To impose a toll upon computer "input" may seriously erode such exemptions for, although no royalty would have to be paid when the material to be used for teaching emerges from the computer, a royalty would be assessed when material was put into the computer. Thus, what is given with one hand would be taken away with the other. It may be that this difficulty cannot be overcome by applying the same exemptions to "input" that are now applicable to "output," for material placed in a computer or an information system may be used in many different ways; probably *some* of those uses should be exempt and others should not be; and it may be impossible to say, at the time the material is placed in the system, to what extent it will be put to exempt uses and to what extent it will be put to nonexempt uses.

Fifth, to charge a toll at the input stage will raise complex and difficult problems when information is transferred from one computer system to another. It may be argued that in such a case there are two inputs, one into the first system and one into the second, but deciding whether such a system is in fact one system composed of many parts or two or more separate systems will also prove difficult. In fact, it is argued, the simplest method of charging a copyright royalty is to charge only for output that takes the form of a reproduction of copyrighted material.

COPYRIGHT PROTECTION FOR COMPUTER PRODUCTS

Programs

Considerable difficulty is encountered in attempting to bootstrap a new technology such as data processing into the traditional areas of law. To use one example, there is as yet no satisfactory definition of "program" which appears adequate for legal purposes. In its final report to the President, the Commission on the Patents described a "program" as follows:

> A series of instructions which control or condition the operation of a data processing machine, generally referred to as a "program," shall not be considered patentable regardless of whether the program is claimed as: (a) an article, (b) a process described in terms of the operations performed by a machine pursuant to a program, or (c) one or more machine configurations established by a program (34).

Still another definition proposed is:

> a computer program is basically a plan that controls the activity of the computer, directing the calculations needed to solve a problem and providing for communication of the solution to the outside world (35).

In its notice setting out the criteria for registration of a computer program, the Copyright Office posed the question and answer:

> What Is a Computer Program?
> In general, a computer program is either a set of operating instructions for a computer or a compilation of reference information to be drawn upon by the computer in solving problems. In most cases the preparation of both of these types of programs involves substantial elements of gathering, choosing, rejecting, editing, and arranging material. Some types of programs also embody verbal material which is written by the programmer and could be considered literary expression (36).

Notwithstanding these legal attempts to describe what it is that causes a computer to do its thing (37), the question of how to handle computer programs under the copyright law remains a twofold subject. The question is twofold since the first aspect is whether programs are a proper subject for copyright; and second, if they are, what is the extent of the protection to be accorded to them.

To take the second aspect first, on the one hand we have the statement of the Deputy Register of Copyrights that:

> Lest any misunderstanding arise, it should be emphasized at the outset that the newly-announced policy [of the Copyright Office in accepting computer programs for registration on May 19, 1964] will not result in protection to the programmer with respect to the idea or system utilized in preparing the program. Copyrights in the program merely protect him against unauthorized copying of that particular program (38).

This lack of protection flows from a basic Supreme Court decision which stated:

> The copyright of a work on mathematical science cannot give to the author an exclusive right to the methods of operation which he propounds, or to the diagrams which he employs to explain them, so as to prevent an engineer from using them whenever occasion requires (39).

Another author has pointed out that the value of a patent or copyright is most dubious:

> In this rapidly developing science, with programs being quickly and continuously outdated by new developments of all kinds, a program's usefulness will frequently be lost long before a judicial dispute about its ownership can be resolved (40).

On the other hand, some others have looked with a most jaundiced eye at the language in the House Report on Copyright Revision which would clearly and unequivocally set a seal of approval upon the register's doubtful decision to admit computer programs to copyright registration. The EDUCOM Task Force in its statement to the Senate Committee considering the Copyright Review Bill painted a most dismal picture should broad protection be extended to computer programs:

> Inclusion of computer programs as possible subjects of copyright immediately raises the all-important question of proper scope of protection to be accorded programs by virtue of copyright. Is it intended that the copyright monopoly shall extend to the use of the program in combination with the computer to attain the result at which the program is aimed? For example, is it proposed that the plan or scheme of running a steel mill or handling payrolls by computer shall become the property of the person who holds the copyright of the program tapes or punch cards which direct the computer, which in turn directs and monitors the operation?
>
> The Revision Bill does not specifically address itself to this problem, but again we are met with broad statutory language defining the proprietor's exclusive rights. The language could conceivably be read as going the whole length of giving an affirmative answer to the foregoing questions—of giving the copyright proprietor of a program ownership of the process, so to speak, which the program embodies. . . .
>
> On principle, the vice in granting copyright to computer programs in the sense of the process is that it would amount to giving programs a breadth of protection similar to that accorded by patent, but without the safeguards and limitations that rightly surround the grant of a patent. Monopoly of systems, schemes, and the like has been granted by our law in the past only under patent, and only upon proof satisfactory to a governmental agency that there has been real 'invention'—a discovery marking a material advance over the prior knowledge. Such a monopoly may last only 17 years. Copyright of a computer program, on the other hand, would be available on the basis of 'originality,' that is, merely an absence of copying without regard to true inventiveness; there would be no serious governmental scrutiny in advance; and the protection would run for a lengthy period of time (the present period is 56 years, and the Revision Bill proposes roughly 75 years). This kind of easy and broad protection for computer programs would threaten to tie up the computer program field and inhibit its progressive development. Had there been such a copyright regime for programs, had programming been constantly carried out under the threat of infringement actions charging plagiarism of existing copyrighted programs, it is doubtful whether the growth of programs and programming techniques of recent years would have been possible. Imagine the condition today if any sizable fraction of the thousands of existing computer programs were held in copyright and copying the processes involved were civilly actionable and even criminally punishable.

The argument has been made in support of, or at least in an apology for, copyright for computer programs covering the processes, that infringement could be avoided simply by changing in some degree the sequence of steps or the problem-solving algorithm of the program. On this view, the presence of a copyright would merely compel an outsider to do some slight work of his own in order to stay out of trouble. The answer to this suggestion is: if copyright of process were accepted, (i) it would make no sense to permit escape from it by trivial variation; (ii) it is very doubtful that courts would take so lighthearted or permissive an attitude toward the infringement question. The tendency of the courts in recent years has been to enlarge rather than to contract the range of actionable plagiarism. Surely it would be most imprudent to assume that courts would be especially gingerly about finding infringement of computer programs, once the basis of protection was established (*41*).

As the EDUCOM statement points out, even *limited* rights regarding copyright protection for computer programs could prove harmful:

If the process embodied in a computer program ought not to be aggrandized through copyright, it might still seem plausible to allow a narrower copyright of a program—one that would confer upon the copyright proprietor the exclusive right to replicate the instructions themselves, the content of the punch cards, tapes, etc., and the right to bar others from making that replication, thereby compelling those others to buy the punch cards, tapes, etc. from the copyright proprietor. But it becomes evident that this right must be carefully circumscribed. For if the outsider is to be assured full access to the process—full right to practice the art comprised in the computer program—then he must be given the accompanying privilege to replicate the program in order to carry out the process or practice the art. Put another way, were the copyright owner of the program empowered to bar the outsider from replicating the program even for the purpose of practicing the art, he would effectively have denied the outsider the ability to practice the art, for the outsider needs to replicate the program or something akin to it in order to instruct his own computer.

On the other hand, the copyright owner of the program might be given the right to prevent others from replicating the content of the punch cards, tapes, etc. simply for the purpose of selling the program on the market or reproducing it in a book on programming. In general, it might not be socially harmful to permit copyright of computer programs limited in scope to replications for purposes other than carrying out the process or practicing the art contained in the programs. Concretely: X prepares a computer program for controlling the production of steel. A copyright of the program by X (obtained on the basis of 'originality') should in no event bar Y, an outsider, from producing steel in the same way, and to that end Y, if he chooses, should be at liberty to replicate X's program exactly. (Of course, Y may prefer to buy the punch cards or tapes from X.) On the other hand Y would not be at liberty to replicate X's program simply to sell copies of it to Z; he would not be permitted to enter into a competition with X in any market that may exist for selling the relevant punch cards, tapes, etc. We imagine this sort of limited copyright in X would not be socially hurtful, although we frankly do not know whether it would be necessary or useful.

Despite the fears expressed above, a more reasonable approach is to conclude that present copyright protections, if any, accorded computer programs, do not extend to the ideas embodied in the program, nor to the techniques used in developing or making the program, nor to "its logical sequence of instructions, which constitute the program's greatest value, but only to the program's format" (42). This follows from the principle enunciated by the Supreme Court in the landmark case of *Baker* v. *Selden* (43):

> The copyright of a work on mathematical science cannot give to the author an exclusive right to the methods of operation which he propounds, or to the diagrams which he employs to explain them, so as to prevent an engineer from using them whenever occasion requires. The very object of publishing a book on science or the useful arts is to communicate to the world the useful knowledge it contains.

This result flows directly from the constitutional provision to "promote the Progress of Science and the useful Arts, by securing for limited Times to Authors and Inventors the exclusive Right to their respective Writings and Discoveries" (44). This very clear language sets forth the footing for our copyright and patent laws, and may be seen to encompass four basic concepts.

First, the primary purpose of the laws is not to reward authors and inventors no matter how deserving or needy; it is not to benefit publishers, printers, or large corporations. The primary purpose of these laws is to *promote the progress of science and the useful arts:* each and every provision of every law promulgated under Article 1, Section 8, has to be in the broad public interest, as enunciated.

The Supreme Court has made it abundantly clear that the benefit to the author is a "secondary consideration" (45), that the primary purpose of copyright is to obtain "the general benefits derived by the public from the labors of authors" (46). In *Mazer* v. *Stein,* the Court set forth the Constitutional rationale:

> The economic philosophy behind the clause empowering Congress to grant patents and copyrights is the conviction that encouragement of individual effort by personal gain is the best way to advance public welfare through the talents of authors and inventors in 'Science and useful Arts' (47).

Even Nimmer, a notable advocate of expanded copyright protections concludes:

> Thus the authorization to grant to individual authors the limited monopoly of copyright is predicated upon the dual premises that the public benefits from the creative activities of authors, and that the copyright monopoly is a necessary condition to the full realization of such creative activities. Implicit in this rationale is the assumption that in the absence of such public benefit the grant of a copyright monopoly to individuals would be unjustified. This appears to be consonant with the pervading public policy against according private economic monopolies in the absence of overriding countervailing considerations [philosophical discussion to the contra omitted] (48).

The second basic concept inherent in the Constitutional language is that the rights given pursuant to copyright and patent legislation must be *for limited times only.* Thus the patent monopoly only extends for 17 years from the date of grant of the patent. And the present basic copyright only extends for 28 years, with a renewal for an additional 28 years. It is certain that the framers of the Constitution, having in mind the many evils under the original English system, while wishing to keep a certain amount of flexibility in a living body of laws, clearly intended to weigh the balance *in favor of unrestricted public access at the earliest possible time.*

A landmark case in the field of patent and copyright law is *Pennock* v. *Dialogue* *(49)*. This case, in discussing the Constitutional Provision against which any proposed patent or copyright law must be measured, stated that this provision "contemplates, therefore, that this right shall exist *but for a limited period,* and that the period shall be subject to the discretion of Congress [emphasis added]" *(50)*. At this time the limited period, albeit for a patent, was for 14 years.

In *Pennock* v. *Dialogue* the Supreme Court early recognized the paramount right of the public in early disclosure and correctly setting out the true rationale of the patent and copyright laws:

> While one great object was, by holding out a reasonable reward to inventors, and giving them an exclusive right to their inventions *for a limited period,* to stimulate the efforts of genius; the main object was 'to promote the progress of science and useful arts;' and this could be done best, by giving the public at large a right to make, construct, use and vend the thing invented, at as early a period as possible, having a due regard to the rights of the inventor. If an inventor should be permitted to hold back from the knowledge of the public the secrets of his invention; if he should, for a long period of years, retain the monopoly, and make and sell his invention publicly, and thus gather the whole profits of it, relying upon his superior skill and knowledge of the structure; and then only, when the danger of competition should force him to secure the exclusive right, he should be allowed to take out a patent, and thus exclude the public from any further use than what should be derived under it, during his fourteen years; it would materially retard the progress of science and the useful arts, and *give a premium to those who should be least prompt to communicate their discoveries* [emphasis added] *(51).*

A third concept provided by the Constitution is that the *authors and inventors* are given a limited monopoly. The Constitution gives no direct rights to the employers of *authors and inventors;* it gives no direct rights to the large corporate body; it does not directly provide for the publisher, the printer, the manufacturer, the football league, and others who form a conduit between the *author or inventor* and the *public.* Therefore, one should conclude that if a present or proposed provision of a Copyright or Patent Law does not clearly provide a direct incentive to the author or inventor so that he will continue his innovative efforts, then that provision is of doubtful validity. Similarly, any incentives which do not serve as a goad to him to continue his creative efforts, although they may provide an economic benefit to the author or inventor, should fail. As just one example, there is no persuasive rationale for bringing live unrehearsed athletic contests under the *copyright umbrella.*

The last, but by no means least concept for copyright, is that it must be a "writing" of an "author" *(52)*. However, Congress and the courts have explicitly expanded the term "writing" far beyond the everyday meaning of actual script, printing, etching, etc., even to nonverbal expressions such as labels, photographs, three-dimensional art forms, and motion pictures; in effect, to all tangible forms of intellectual creation. Banzhaff suggests three prerequisites: "permanence, tangibility, and a form capable of being copied" (53), and argues that computer programs meet these physical requirements. The Copyright Office was much more hesitant in deciding whether to accept computer programs for registration:

> The registrability of computer programs involves two basic questions: (1) Whether a program as such is the "writing of an author" and thus copyrightable, and (2) whether a reproduction of the program in a form actually used to operate or be "read" by a machine is a "copy" that can be accepted for copyright registration.
>
> Both of these are doubtful questions. However, in accordance with its policy of resolving doubtful issues in favor of registration wherever possible, the Copyright Office will consider registration for a computer program if certain requirements have been met. . . .
>
> Registration for a computer program will be considered if:
> (a) The elements of assembling, selecting, arranging, editing, and literary expression that went into the compilation of the program are sufficient to constitute original authorship.
> (b) The program has been published, with the required copyright notice; that is, "copies" (i.e., reproductions of the program in a form perceptible or capable of being made perceptible to the human eye) bearing the notice have been distributed or made available to the public.
> (c) The copies deposited for registration consist of or include reproductions in a language intelligible to human beings. If the first publication was in a form (such as machine-readable tape) that cannot be perceived visually or read by humans, something more (such as a print-out of the entire program) must be deposited along with two complete copies of the program as first published . . . (36).

Here it is well to remember that statutory copyright in a published work is obtained by publication with notice of copyright (54). Registration by the Copyright Office does not create the copyright, but merely records it (54).

Further, it has been held that the Register has a broad, but not unlimited, area of discretion in determining what subject matter, in his opinion, is copyrightable, and thus acceptable for registration (55). "However, the courts will generally treat with great weight the actual practices of the Copyright Office" (56).

However, despite the traditional weight given the Register of Copyright's determination as to what is registerable, hence copyrightable, most commentators would not attach extreme importance either way to the Copyright Office's consideration of programs for registration, particularly in view of the Register's statement that at best registerability is a doubtful question. Ultimate resolution must await judicial and/or legislative determination.

The physical form of the program presents additional difficulty. As noted above, in its initial announcement the Copyright Office required a printed or visible form such as a machine listing or flowchart "of the complete program."

One commentator in fact concluded:

> The other physical forms that a computer program may assume present a more difficult problem. On the basis of existing procedure, a punched deck of cards or

> tape, a roll of magnetic tape, or similar representations, would probably be denied copyright protection. In and of themselves such forms of information are meaningless to the average reader. Even giving a most sweeping interpretation to *Burrow-Giles Lithographic Co.* v. *Sarony,* which rejected a literary interpretation of the term "writing" in the "copyright clause" of the United States Constitution, one would not likely consider a pile of perforated cards, a few yards of sievelike paper tape, or a magnetized tape to be a "writing" of an author [footnotes omitted] (57).

However, once more the ugly facts of life intruded in the first year of registration of computer programs. Of the sixteen claims covering programs, thirteen consisted of printouts only. In two cases, punched cards with full interpretation at the top were accepted. In one instance, magnetic tape without a complete printout was accepted:

> Since the program on magnetic tape could not be perceived visually or read, it was necessary that a print-out be deposited also. The deposit of magnetic tape presented additional difficulties in view of the size of the particular program; the applicant said that a print-out of the entire program would be approximately 12 feet high. To resolve the problem the reels of tape were deposited along with selected portions of the print-out namely, *the beginning of the work* including the title and the copyright notice, *part of the center,* and *the end* [emphasis added] (58).

In conclusion therefore, it may be said that the copyrightability of computer programs is doubtful; however, deposit for registration with the Register of Copyrights may be had, and the form of the program deposited need not be visible to the unaided human eye.

Computer Produced Output

Another area of controversy, as yet unillumed by either statute or court decision, is the protection accorded computer produced output. Thus annual contests are held for computer-derived drawings and other works of art (59). As mentioned above, computer-generated concordances, bibliographies, indices, and other literary materials are becoming more and more common. Here too the enthusiasm of the dedicated is most contagious:

> Since the electronic computer was invented, its usefulness to society has been limited more by the imagination of man than by the capability of the hardware. The possibility of a computer creating music, art, or literature is perhaps obscure only because our pride forces us to believe these areas are man's exclusive provinces.
>
> At the 1966 Fall Joint Computer Conference, Professor Heinz Von Foerster organized a highly creative, imaginative and enjoyable session on "Computers in Music." The papers presented at the session were received with great enthusiasm; and form the basis of this book. The ideas advanced here may well lead to exciting and publicly accepted music of the future (60).

Roughly speaking, three possible contributions by the computer to music may be expected—and by analogy to other art or literary works: (1) Generation of acoustic tones, (2) melodic and rhythmic composition, and (3) execution of a composition without a human performer/orchestra.

Obviously (1) and (3) are important; witness the hit parade success of the recent Moog Synthesized version of Bach. However, only (2) need be of concern in considering copyright or literary protection. The Copyright Office has already received works for registration allegedly created by computer: musical compositions, abstract drawings, and compilations of various sorts. Here they feel the test will be the human element involved: "whether the 'work' is basically one of human authorship, with the computer merely being an assisting instrument, or whether the traditional elements of authorship in the work (literary, artistic, or musical expression or elements of selection, arrangement, etc.) were actually conceived and executed not by man but by a machine" (61). It is somewhat paradoxical but accurate to contemplate that the more successful the computer creation is the less likely it is that the result will be copyrightable (62).

The distinction between the author or producer of stored material and the user of the material in large computer utility operations is already blurred (63). As noted in our introduction, the user is becoming a part of the writing itself:

> One is reminded of "aleatoric" music in which the line between performer and composer wavers. Professor McLuhan, a professional soothsayer, says broadly that as the imperium in communications passes from books to electronic manifestations, as the "Gutenberg galaxy" decays, not only is the relationship between author and audience radically changed but the author's pretensions to individual ownership and achievement are at a discount: his dependence on the past is better appreciated; he is seen somewhat as a tradition-bearing "singer of tales," as a kind of teacher peculiarly indebted to his teachers before him. (I suppose claims of exempt status for educational uses of copyrighted works dimly reflect such an idea.) [Footnote omitted.] (64)

So far, at least, the computer has not invaded the provinces of artistic and literary endeavor to the same extent that it has revolutionized scientific fields. But already the use of computers is impacting the former areas, transforming what was a barrier between technology and creativity into a partnership. As noted above, in music the computer can be a source of sound or a means of composition. Sound can be converted mathematically into light patterns. The machines can already produce a most vivid prose or poetic work.

In addition, this new tool is bringing the engineer and scientist directly into aesthetic creativity on all fronts. In 1968 an historic exhibition, entitled "Cybernetic Serendipity," was held in London and toured the United States in 1969. This exhibition, and its accompanying catalog (65), "surveys the present state of accomplishment in the creation of artistic forms through technological means by experimenters all over the world" (66). It remains to be seen what, if any, legal protections are necessary or will be devised to maintain peace with this new "organic interrelation" and "organic interdependence" where the intake of information fuses with the consumption of the creative enlightenment (67).

Nimmer indicates two requirements that a work must meet to constitute a "writing," i.e., to become eligible for copyright: (1) tangible form and (2) intellectual labor. He further indicates that the "intellectual labor" standard may also be required by the concept of "author" (*68*).

This would follow from the *Trademark Cases* (*69*) where the Supreme Court held that a trademark does not constitute a "writing" in the copyright sense; a result consistent with the notion that the value imputed to a trademark is based upon market acceptance for product identification. That is, trademark rights flow from the *use* and only the *use* of the mark—*not* the originality or intellectual creativity involved in selecting the mark (*70*).

Thus, in trying to ascertain whether a computer result is a "writing" of a [human] "author" one must make a judgment as to whether:

> the intellectual labor expended [by the human] in its creation is so trivial as to be virtually non-existent . . . a very slight degree of [intellectual] labor will be sufficient to qualify the work as a writing in the constitutional sense. Thus, almost any ingenuity [by a human] is selection [possibly from multiple outputs], combination or expression, no matter how crude, humble or obvious, will be sufficient to render the work a "writing" (*71*).

"FAIR USE" AS IT AFFECTS THE COMPUTER AND INFORMATION SCIENTIST

One of the most prickly ideas to permeate the field of literary protections is the concept of "fair use."

Briefly stated, "fair use" may be defined as the permissable "use"—copying or performance—of a copyrighted work over the *objection, express or implied,* of the copyright proprietor (*72*):

> If there is anything absolute about fair use, it is that it is a concept favoring the user of the copyrighted work and not the owner. It limits the rights of the copyright owner. It has served as a reasonable safety valve to the almost paralytic effect that copyright might have placed on the sensible use and exploitation of published works, if the law had been interpreted as an absolute doctrine. Even the copyright owner recognizes this (*73*).

In its report on the Copyright Revision Bill (*74*), the House Judiciary Committee accurately noted that "although the courts have considered and ruled upon the fair use doctrine over and over again, no real definition of the concept has ever emerged. Indeed, since the doctrine is *an equitable rule of reason,* no generally applicable definition is possible, and each case raising the question must be decided on its own facts" (*75*). Further, the concept "fair use" only comes into play when one is sued for copyright infringement, and raises the affirmative defense that the particular use made is not an infringement but is permitted over the wishes of the copyright proprieter, i.e., it is a fair use.

Nimmer has suggested that the distinction between fair use and infringement may rest upon the question as to whether or not the defendant's use "tends to diminish or prejudice the sale of the plaintiff's work. . . . if regardless of medium, the defendent's work . . . performs a different function than that of the plaintiff's, the defense of fair use may be involved" (76).

In its report, the House Committee noted four criteria for balancing the equities, and included these criteria in its version of the Copyright Revision Bill for the first statuatory recognition of the doctrine (77). However, the committee emphasized that its specific language was "intended to restate the present judicial doctrine of fair use, not to change, narrow, or enlarge it in any way" (77). Thus, the committee's definition of "fair use" and the relevant criteria may be considered a basis for establishing workable practices and policies:

> . . . the fair use of a copyrighted work . . ., for purposes such as criticism, comment, news reporting, teaching, scholarship, or research, is not an infringement of copyright. In determining whether the use made of a work in any particular case is a fair use, the factors to be considered shall include—
>
> (1) The purpose and character of the use;
>
> (2) the nature of the copyrighted work;
>
> (3) the amount and substantiality of the portion used in relation to the copyrighted work as a whole; and
>
> (4) the effect of the use upon the potential market for or value of the copyrighted work.

Therefore, one may reasonably conclude that *at present* inclusion of copyrighted material within a computer-based information retrieval system, as described earlier, would constitute fair use, even though changes were made for and profits were realized from the output of the computer system (78). If the technology and economics develop so that such activities constitute an actual rather than potential threat to traditional copyright uses, then a contrary result may occur, especially if the courts do not find an overwhelming social policy in favor of the new technology (79).

CONCLUSIONS

Many intriguing and interesting questions are beyond the scope of this discussion other than in a most cursory fashion.

Antitrust

If computer programs are able to be protected by copyright or patent, then they no longer may be offered on a package basis, but must be offered separately on reasonable terms, i.e., there is a per se antitrust rule prohibiting tie-in arrangements since the latter "serve no useful purpose except to retain competition" (80).

Copyright owners may not act together to extend their individual monopolies without running afoul of the antitrust laws (81).

Similarly, it is most doubtful on antitrust grounds whether a dominant computer manufacturer may refuse to sell a copyrighted program (82) or restrict its use to a given central processor in the absence of a strong pro-competitive rationale (83).

Future Prospects

At the time of this writing, it seems most unlikely that the long-awaited Copyright Revision Bill will be enacted unless there is some legislative fluke. There appears to be unanimous agreement that the drafters of the Copyright Revision Bill in particular were ignorant of "the technological and policy problems posed by computers" (*84*). Whether or not a proposed commission will study these problems also seems problematical, in light of the opposition, albeit justified, of certain groups (*55*).

Kaplan has painted a vivid picture of the future of copyright in the new computer-bred technological environment:

> You must imagine, at the eventual heart of things to come, linked or integrated systems or networks of computers capable of storing faithful simulacra of the entire treasure of the accumulated knowledge and artistic production of past ages, and of taking into the store new intelligence of all sorts as produced. The systems will have a prodigious capacity for manipulating the store in useful ways, for selecting portions of it upon call and transmitting them to any distance, where they will be converted as desired to forms directly or indirectly cognizable, whether as printed pages, phonorecords, tapes, transient displays of sights or sounds, or hieroglyphs for further machine uses. Lasers, microwave channels, satellites improving on Comsat's Early Bird, and, no doubt, many devices now unnamable, will operate as ganglions to extend the reach of the systems to the ultimate users as well as to provide a copious array of additional services.
>
> Conceived as conduits or highways for the transmission of signals, the systems will have intense responsibilities of a "public utility" type enforced by law if indeed the systems (or some of them) will not come under direct government ownership and control. Horrors of Orwellian dimensions lurk in far-reaching official regulation of the communications pattern; but to say that is merely to sound a summons to wise public regulation. If the systems will have public duties, so will new intellectual productions once unbosomed and released by the authors— the duties of submitting themselves to deposit in some form appropriate for archival purposes and to permit any manipulations of indexing, abstracting, and so forth needed to connect them, to key them in, with the existing store. This contribution made by new works need not involve their exposure to full-length use by unwelcome clients. At present, self-interest on the part of authors and publishers has usually resulted in adequate public access to works, and the law has rarely had to become insistent. Probably the law of the future will lose patience rather quickly with the mere idiosyncratic withholding of access. But I should hope there will ever be play for the humane development of the "moral rights" of authors to prevent abuses in the exploitation of their creations. This will indeed be especially important if copyright itself recedes as a significant control.
>
> Copyright is likely to recede, to lose relevance, in respect to most kinds of uses of a great amount of scholarly production which now sees light in a melange of learned journals and in the output of university presses. In the future little of this will ever be published in conventional book or journal form. . . .
>
> . . . For many of the uses available through the machine, exaction of copyright payments will be felt unnecessary to provide incentive or headstart—especially so, when the works owe their origin, as so many will, to one or another kind of public support.
>
> I am suggesting that copyright or the larger part of its controls will appear unneeded, merely obstructive, as applied to certain sectors of production and that

here copyright law will lapse into disuse and may disappear. For the rest, copyright will persist to serve its historic purposes. For various early, prime exploitations of particular new works, whether or not accomplished through the electronic systems, there will be individual accountings, with separate financial hazards and successes or failures. The secondary and later exploitations will be largely through the systems. . . .

But what is suggested, on more sober reflection, is methods by which large repertories of works will be made available for a great variety of uses, and charges and remittances figured on a rough-and-ready basis, all with liberal application of some principle of "clearance at the source" to prevent undue bother down the line to the final consumer.

Unless, indeed, the systems are set up by government direct, government will probably intervene to establish fair standards for admission of works into the systems, for giving potential users access to the systems, for figuring rates, for making distributions to copyright owners. But under conditions of extensive government concern with the operations of the systems, which will have become supremely facile and widely encompassing of the transmission of intelligence, it may appear sensible to displace copyright and substitute other, perhaps more direct, encouragements to original production. We may in any case expect legislators of the future to regard copyright as only one among a number of expedients for stimulating creativity (86).

Copyright already is affecting and being affected by the computer revolution. Historically, it developed as "a private concept by a private group." It resulted in a "rigidity" springing from "the application of rules without guiding principles" which in turn resulted from the courts construing "a statute for a particular purpose: to destroy an opprobrious monopoly."

"Copyright [is] not a product of the common law." [The courts did not see it as "a concept used to deal with exceedingly complex issues, issues which require careful distinctions based upon a perceptive awareness of the problems, an understanding of purpose, and an appreciation of function."] "It was a product of censorship, guild monopoly, trade regulation statutes, and misunderstanding" (87).

In a society where machines compute at the speed of light (88), where man visits the moon on live color television, and where wars are termed "happenings, tragic games" (89), much of the traditional protection of invisible property vis copyright seems obsolescent if not obscene. It remains to be seen whether society is well or ill-served by retaining the placebo termed copyright.

PROTECTING PROPRIETARY RIGHTS IN SOFTWARE: A BIBLIOGRAPHY

There is an increasing interest in the extent to which proprietary rights in software—computer programs—may or should be protected by formal legal means, whether traditional or innovative.

In order to give a ready access to the literature, the attached bibliography has been compiled of references known to the author as of December 1968. Many of the references were first given in his bibliography on "Law, Logic, and the Computer" which appeared in *Computing Reviews*. (Single copies of the latter are available without charge from the Association for Computing Machinery, 211 East 43rd Street, New York, N.Y. 10017, request Bibliographics 9, 13, and 22.)

Background materials selected for this summation of necessity represent the compiler's personal preferences. Thus, no attempt is made to give general articles dealing with trade secrets, contracts, or infringements. No impression is meant or should be taken that the law in this area is well-defined or developed. To the contrary, by and large there are no statutes, cases, or decisions that directly confront the problems. The writings in the field deal almost entirely with analogies and examples from nonrelated areas. Hence the conclusions drawn therefrom should be viewed with a substantial amount of skepticism, particularly when the "solutions" would affront common sense, current business practice, or the public interest.

A special note of appreciation for their aid in this compilation is given to Mrs. Evelyn Abbott and Mrs. Karen Carsrud.

This work was supported in part by a grant from the National Science Foundation. However, responsibility for the accuracy and completeness rests solely with the compiler.

1. Aarons, L. F., "Poser: Is Computer a Citizen?" [Copyright of Machine Produced Creative Efforts], *Washington Post,* April 20, 1966, p. C7.

2. Almon, W. J. (Chairman), R. Freed, J. Moshman, J. A. Larkin, and M. Allen. Legal responsibilities of computer people" [Panel], 1965 ACM Conference, Cleveland, Ohio, August 26, 1965.

3. Awalt, F. G., Jr., "Computer Contract," in *Computers and the Law* (R. P. Bigelow, ed.), American Bar Assoc., Chicago, 1966, pp. 40–47.

4. Awalt, F. G., Jr., "Corporate Law Aspects of Computers," in *Computers and the Law* (R. P. Bigelow, ed.), American Bar Assoc., Chicago, 1966, pp. 85–89.

5. Awalt, F. G., Jr., "Corporate Legal Problems Associated with Computers," *Modern Uses of Logic in Law,* **1965**, 99–115 (September).

6. Awalt, F. G., Jr., "Lawyer's Concern with a Computer Installation," *Business Lawyer,* **21**, 381–400 (January 1966).

7. Bachard, R. A., "Patents: Proposed Guidelines to Examination of Programs," *Tulsa Law J.,* **1967**, 258–262 (June).

8. Banzhaf, J. F., III, "Copyrighted Computer Programs: Some Questions and Answers," *Comput. Autom.,* **14**, 22–25 (July 1965).

9. Banzhaf, J. F., III, "Legal Protection for Computer Programs," *Columbia Law Rev.,* **64**, 1274–1300 (November 1964) [CR Rev. 8093].

10. Banzhaf, J. F., III, "Of Lawyers and Computers" [Report on 1965 ALI Conference, New York], *Datamation,* **11**, 142 (May 1965).

11. Banzhaf, J. F., III, "On Computers and Programs; Copyrights and Patents," *Comm. ACM,* **8**, 220 (April 1965) [CR Rev. 8094].

12. Banzhaf, J. F., III, "Legal Protection for Computer Programs," *Data Proc. Mag.,* **7**, 8–12 (July 1964).

13. Banzhaf, J. F., III, "Statement of Position before Subcommittee No. 3 of the House Judiciary Committee" [Copyright Protection for Computer Programs, and Use of Copyrighted Material in Information Storage and Retrieval Systems], *Comput. Autom.,* **14**, 9–27 (September 1965); **14**, 10–11 (October 1965).

14. Banzhaf, J. F., III, "Copyright Protection for Computer Programs," in *Proc. 1st Law of Software Conf., Washington, D.C., October 1968* (I. Kayton, ed.), George Washington Univ., Washington, D.C., 1968, pp. C-33–C-51.

15. Banzhaf, J. F., III, "Computers and Copyright Law: A Commentary" [Letter], *Comm. ACM,* **10**, 61 (January 1967).

16. Banzhaf, J. F., III, "Copyright Law Revision: A Recent Amendment Favors Information Storage and Retrieval—A Report to the Data Processing Community" [Letter to Editor], *Comput. Autom.,* **15,** 10–11 (December 1966).

17. Banzhaf, J. F., III, A. Bogsch, L. I. Boonin, E. C. Gonda, M. C. Jacobs, C. J. C. McOustra (Chairman), and M. R. Wessel, "Legal Protection for Computer Programs," *Computer J.,* **8,** 289–296 (January 1966) [CR Rev. 11,756].

18. Baram, M. S., "Trade Secrets: What Price Loyalty," *Harvard Business Rev.,* **46,** 66–74 (November–December 1968).

19. Barr, R., "Copyright Proposal Draws No Cheers," *Electronic News,* **1967,** 34 (April 10).

20. Barr, R., "Patent Row Resumes—Hit Senate Bill on Software Exclusion," *Electronic News,* **1968,** 1, 18 (February 5).

21. Barr, R., "Program Patenting Seen Likely," *Electronic News,* **1968,** Sec. 2, 46 (April 29).

22. Bell, T. K., "Industrial Espionage: Privacy of Secret Scientific and Technical Information," *U.C.L.A. Law Rev.,* **14,** 911–934 (March 1967).

23. Bender, D., "Business and Research Data on Software Development," *Proc. 1st Law of Software Conf., Washington, D.C., October 1968* (I. Kayton, ed.), George Washington Univ., Washington, D.C. 1968, pp. A-15–A-43.

24. Bender, D., "Computer Programs: Should They Be Patentable?," *Columbia Law Rev.,* **68,** 241–259 (February 1968).

25. Bender, D., "Single Pricing for Hardware and Software," in *Proc. 1st Law of Software Conf., Washington, D.C., October 1968* (I. Kayton, ed.), George Washington Univ., Washington, D.C. 1968, D-1–D-23.

26. Bender, D., and C. G. Benjamin, "Impact of New Technology on the Economy of Specialized Publications," in *Proc. 1st Law of Software Conf., Washington, D.C., October 1968* (I. Kayton, ed.), George Washington Univ., Washington, D.C., 1968, pp. C-1–C-14.

27. Bigelow, R. P., "Legal Aspects of Proprietary Software," *Datamation,* **14,** 32–39 (October 1968).

28. Boonin, L. I., "Patents and Copyrights—What Should be Protected?" (1965 IFIP Cong., New York), *Comm. ACM,* **8,** 474 (July 1965).

29. Brady, R. F., "Copyrights Patents," *Datamation,* **11,** 2–12 (February 1965).

30. Brennan, T. C., "S. 2216, to Establish the National Commission on New Technological Uses of Copyrighted Works," *Bull. Copyright Soc.,* **15,** 24–28 (October 1967).

31. Brenner, E. J., "Future of Computer Programs in the U.S. Patent Office," in *Proc. 1st Law of Software Conf., Washington, D.C., October 1968* (I. Kayton, ed.), George Washington Univ., Washington, D.C. 1968, pp. B-1–B-23.

32. Brown, W., "Computers and Patents and Industrial Secrets," Presented at Law of Computers Symposium, Ann Arbor, Michigan, June 7–8, 1968.

33. Cary, G., "Copyright Registration and Computer Programs," *Bull. Copyright Soc.,* **11,** 362 (August 1964).

34. Cary, G., "Registrability of Computer Programs," in *Proc. 1st Law of Software Conf., Washington, D.C., October 1968* (I. Kayton, ed.), George Washington Univ., Washington, D.C. 1968, pp. C-15–C-31.

35. Clampett, H. A., Jr., "Program Patents—Yea or Nay," *Datamation,* **13,** 140 (December 1967).

36. Connally, R., and H. David, "U.S. Court Finds Softwear [sic] Patentable in Landmark Case," *Electronic News,* **1968,** 2 (November 25).

37. Dansiger, S. J., "Proprietary Protection of Computer Programs," *Comput. Auto.,* **17,** 32 (February 1968).

38. Davidson, L., "Practical Considerations in Program Patentability," *Comput. Auto.,* **17,** 12–13 (May 1968).

39. de Sola Pool, I., "Social Trends" [Changed by Communications Revolution] [Including Copyright], *Sci, Technol.,* **1968,** 87–101 (April).

40. Detmer, J. M., and B. I. Savage, "Copyrighted Computer Programs: Some Comments," *Comput. Autom.,* **14,** 13, 56 (December 1965).

41. Dorn, W. F., R. L. Lowry, W. B. Ross, and R. Wilson, "Intergovernmental Interface. A Panel Discussion on the Problems of Data Classification, Shared Responsibility for Program Administration, and the Proprietary Nature of Data" [Panel], 1967 NYU Local Government Conf., June 21, 1967.

42. Duggan, M. A., "Report on the Copywright [sic] Situation," *Comm. ACM,* **11,** 458 (June 1968).

43. Elgroth, G. V., "Patentability and Forging Practice Relating to Computer Programming," Paper presented at Federal Bar Association Session on Legal Protection of Computer Programming, Washington, D.C., September 1968.

44. Encke, F. L., and E. H. Sheers, "Copyright of Patents for Computer Programs?," *J. Patent Office Soc.,* **49,** 323–327 (May 1967).

45. Etienne, A. J., and M. D. Goldberg, "Patent and Copyright Implications of Electronic Data Processing," in *Proceedings, 8th Annual Public Conference, IDEA,* **8,** 176–201 (1964— Conf. No.).

46. Freed, R. N., "Effect of Computer Technology on Legal Liability," *Corporate Law: Proceedings of Wisconsin's Eighth Annual Corporate Lawyer's Institute,* 1962, p. 49.

47. Freed, R. N., "Legal Caveats and Pitfalls in Data Processing," in *1966 American Management Association EDP Conference, New York, March 2, 1966.*

48. Freed, R. N., "Legal Implications of Computer Use," Paper presented at ACM Natl. Cong., Syracuse, New York, September 4–7, 1962 [and as "Legal Implications of the Computer Revolution, *Comm. ACM,* **5,** 607–612 (1962)]. [Under the latter title in *Proc. 1962 ACM Natl. Cong.,* p. 40.] [CR Rev. 3026.]

49. Frishauf, S. H., *Industrial Protection of Computer Programs—Bibliography,* New York, (1966), 3 pp., mimeographed. Available from Michael A. Duggan.

50. Galler, B. A., and C. N. Mooers, "Language Protection by Trademark Ill-advised; and Reply," *Comm. ACM,* **11,** 148–149 (March 1968).

51. Gee, R. D., "Computers and Copyright," *Comput. Bull.,* **9,** 1 (September 1965).

52. Goetz, M. A., U.S. Patent No. 3,380,029, "Sorting System "[software], Filed April 9, 1965; Granted April 23, 1968.

53. Goetz, M. A., "Proprietary Programs—Can They Break the Software Monopoly?," *Data Processing Mag.,* **10,** 48–49 (January 1968).

54. Goldberg, D., "Patent and Copyright Implications of Electronic Data Processing," *IDEA,* **8,** 183 (1964).

55. Goldberg, M. D. (Chairman), "Computers and Copyright: New Technology and Revision of the Old Law: Symposium," *Bull. Copyright Soc.,* **15,** 1–3 (October 1967).

56. Goodwin, N., *Information Processing Systems and Copyright Legislation,* Goodwin, Rosenbau, Meachan & White, Washington, D.C., 1966, mimeographed; private distribution.

57. Gosness, C. F., "Copying Grab Bag: Observations on the New Copyright Legislation," *Amer. Lib. Assoc. Bull.,* **64,** 46–55 (January 1966).

58. Graves, E. M. (Chairman), D. M. Lacey, L. Loevinger, and J. Schulman, "Information Explosion: Panel," At Meeting of the American Patent Law Assoc., Washington, D.C., January 24, 1967; *Amer. Patent Law Assoc. Bull.,* **1967,** 51–87 (January–February).

59. Greenbaum, A. J., "Computers, Copyrights, and the Law Prior to Revision," *Bull. Copyright Soc.,* **15,** 164 (February 1968).

60. Haanstra, J. W., "Software—An Independent Existence?," in *Proc. 1st Law of Software Conf., Washington, D.C., October 1968* (I. Kayton, ed.), George Washington Univ., Washington, D.C., 1968, pp. A-1–A-13.

61. Hamann, H. F., "Copyright Aspects of Automatic Information Storage and Retrieval Systems," *Bull. Copyright Soc.,* **15,** 9–12 (October 1967).

62. Hamburger, A., U.S. Patent No. 3,333,243, "Detection and Correction of Transposition Errors" [software disguised as hardware], Filed September 16, 1963; Granted July 25, 1967.

63. Hamlin, K. B., "Computer Programs are Patentable," *Comm. ACM,* **7,** 581 (October 1964).

64. Hamlin, K. B., "Patentability of Computer Programs under Present Statutes," Paper presented at FBA Session on Legal Protection of Computer Programming, Washington, D.C., September 1968.

65. Hauptman, G. A., "Joint Inventorship of Computers," *Comm. ACM,* **7,** 579 (October 1964).

66. Heilprin, L. B., "Technology and the Future of the Copyright Principle, *Amer. Doc.,* **19,** 6–11 (January 1968).

67. Henry, D. S., "Legal Problems in Connection with the Use of Electronic Equipment," *Proc. Assoc. Life Ins. Counsel,* **14,** 243 (1958).

68. Hill, J., "Scope of Protection for Computer Programs under the Copyright Law," *De Paul Law Rev.,* **14,** 360–370 (1965).

69. Hirsch, P., "Patent Office Examines Software: Guidelines Get Graded Down" [Patenting of Programs], *Datamation,* **12,** 79, 81 (November 1966).

70. Hoefler, D. C., "Patent Reform Briefing Ignites Alarm, Dismay," *Electronic News,* **1967,** 12 (March 13).

71. Hoffman, P. S., "Contracts for Computers: Economic Considerations," in *Computers and the Law* (R. P. Bigelow, ed.), American Bar Assoc., Chicago, 1966, pp. 39–40.

72. Holt, J. F., "Software Copyrights," *Datamation,* **11,** 13 (April 1965).

73. Horty, J. F., "Computers and Copyright: A Third Area," *Bull. Copyright Soc.,* **15,** 19–23 (October 1967).

74. Jacobs, M. C., "Patent Protection of Computer Programs," *Comm. ACM,* **7,** 583 (October 1964).

75. Jacobs, M. C., "Patent, Copyright, and Trade Secret Aspects of Computers, in *Computers and the Law* (R. P. Bigelow, ed.), American Bar Assoc., Chicago, 1966, pp. 90–93.

76. Jacobs, M. C., "Patent Protection of Computer Programs," *J. Patent Office Soc.,* **47,** 6–14 (January 1965).

77. Jacobs, M. C., "Legal Protection of Computer Software" [Panel], AFIPS Conference, Atlantic City, New Jersey, April 20, 1967.

78. Jacobs, M. C. "[President's], Commission's [on Patent System] Report" (Re: Computer Programs), *J. Patent Office Soc.,* **49,** 372–378 (May 1967).

79. Jacobs, M. C., "Patentable Machines—Systems Embodiable Either in Software or Hardware," in *Proc. 1st Law of Software Conf., Washington, D.C., October 1968* (I. Kayton. ed.), George Washington Univ., Washington, D.C., 1968, pp. B-77–B-93.

80. Jacobs, M. C., "Trade Secrets, Antitrust and Other Aspects of Computer Programming," Paper presented at Federal Bar Association Session on Legal Protection of Computer Programming, Washington, D.C., September 1968.

81. Jones, R. C., "Jones of ADR Testifies in Support of Software Patents," *Comm. ACM,* **11,** 210 (March 1968).

82. Jones, R. C., "Programs and Software Should be Patentable—Statement Submitted February 1, 1968, to Senate Subcommittee on Patents & Copyrights," *Comput. Auto.,* **17,** 11, 12 (March 1968).

83. Kates, J. P., "Computer Patent Disclosures," *Comm. ACM,* **7,** 578 (October 1964).

84. Katona, G. P., "Legal Protection of Computer Programs," *J. Patent Office Soc.,* **47,** 955–979 (December 1965).

85. Kayton, I., "Patent Protectability of Software: Background and Current Law," in *Proc. 1st Law of Software Conf., Washington, D.C., October 1968* (I. Kayton, ed.), George Washington Univ., Washington, D.C., 1968, pp. B-25–B-53.

86. Keough, W. H., "Computers . . . Some Legal Aspects," *NAA Bull.,* **45,** 21–26 (February 1964).

87. Koller, H. R., "Patent Protection for Computer Software: Implications for the Industry," in *Proc. 1st Law of Software Conf., Washington, D.C., October 1968* (I. Kayton, ed.), George Washington Univ., Washington, D.C., 1968, p. A-45.

88. Kornblum, R. D., "New Voice for the Chorus" [Use of Copyright Materials in an Automated IR System], *Business Autom.,* **12,** 98 (June 1965).

89. Kurtz, R. E., "Patents and Data Processing," *Data Processing,* **6,** 9–13 (November 1964).

90. Lardner, G., Jr., "Data Center Hearing Warned on Privacy," *Washington Post,* July 27, 1966, pp. A1, A8.

91. Lauder, F. H., "Copyright Aspects of Computer Usage," *Comm. ACM,* **7,** 572 (October 1964); *Bull. Copyright Soc.,* **11,** 380 (August 1964).

92. Lauro, M. J., "Proprietary Data" [Letter re Suit on Employee Restrictions When Leaving Employ], *Aviation Week,* **86,** 118 (April 1967).

93. Lawlor, R. C., "Bibliography re Patent and Copyright Law in Relation to Computer Technology," *Modern Uses of Logic in Law,* **1965,** 53–55 (June).

94. Lawlor, R. C., "Literary Property and Computer Technology," in *Proc. 1966 ACM Conf., Los Angeles, September 1, 1966.*

95. Lawlor, R. C., "Information Retrieval and Copyright Law Revision" [Presented at 3rd Technical Conf. of the Council of the Social Science Data Archives, Ann Arbor, Michigan, May 10–12, 1966], *Social Sciences Information,* **6,** 75–85 (February 1967).

96. Lieb, C. H., "Computer and Copyright the Next Five Years. Summary of Proceedings, Section of Patent, Trademark and Copyright Law," *Amer. Bar Assoc. J.,* **1967,** 132–136 (August). Also in *Bull. Copyright Soc.,* **15** (October 1967).

97. Linden, B., "Book Publishing," Presented at 1967 American University Copyright Law Revision Symposium, Washington, D.C., April 20, 1967.

98. Lorinczi, G. C., "When Does the Computer Engage in Unauthorized Practice," *Amer. Bar Assoc. J.,* **54,** 379–381 (April 1968). Also in *Law Comput. Technol.,* **1,** 10–13 (July 1968) [CR Rev. 14,660].

99. Marke, J. J., "Commentary on the Report: 'Intellectual Property and Copyright Law,'" Presented at 1967 American University Copyright Law Revision Symposium, Washington, D.C., April 20, 1967.

100. Marke, J. J., *Copyright and Intellectual Property,* Report to the Fund for the Advancement of Education, New York, January 1967, 112 pp.

101. Marke, J. J., "Copyright Revisited," *Wilson Lib. Bull., 42,* 35–45 (September 1967).

102. Markham, J. W., "Economic Analysis of the New Information Technologies," in *Economic-media Study of Book Publishing,* 1966, pp. 1–30.

103. Messenheimer, A. D. (Program Moderator), Federal Bar Association Session on the Legal Protection of Computer Programming, Washington, D.C., September 1968.

104. Miller, A. R., "Computers and Copyright Law," *Michigan State Bar J., 46,* 11 (April 1967).

105. Miller, A. R., "Computers and Copyrights," Presented at Law of Computers Symposium, Ann Arbor, Michigan, June 7–8, 1968.

106. Miller, A. R., "Copyright Revision Bill in Relation to Computers (Prepared for EDUCOM)," *Comm. ACM, 10,* 318–321 (May 1967).

107. Miller, A. R., "Legal Implications of the Use of Computers—A Brief Overview," Presented at Law of Computers Symposium, Ann Arbor, Michigan, June 7–8, 1968.

108. Moore, J. A., "Programmers and Unions [Letter], *Datamation, 11,* 12 (June 1965).

109. Mott, L. E., U.S. Patent No. 3,319,226, "Data Processor Module for a Modular Data Processing System for Execution of Multi-tasks and Multi-programs," [Variable length instruction acceptance; multilevel operated stock; single and multiple indexing relative and indirect addressing; subroutine control and interrupt system], Filed November 30, 1962; Granted May 9, 1967.

110. Mumford, L. Q., "Administrative Developments: Registrability of Computer Programs," in *Annual Report of the Librarian of Congress, 1964,* Govt. Printing Office, Washington, D.C., 1965, p. 79.

111. Mumford, L. Q., "Administrative Developments: Problems Arising from Computer Technology," in *Annual Report of the Librarian of Congress, 1965,* Govt. Printing Office, Washington, D.C., 1966, pp. 84–85, 91.

112. McOustra, C. J. C. (Organizer), "Panel on Legal Aspects on Computer Software," 1965 IFIP Congress, New York.

113. McOustra, C. J. C., "Software: Copyright and Other Kinds of Control," *Comput. Bull., 8,* 96 (December 1964).

114. Nelson, G. J., "Copyrightability of Computer Programs," *Arizona Law Rev., 7,* 204–218 (Spring 1966).

115. Neville, H. G., "Data Processing Insurance," *Data Process Mgmt., 5,* 35 (October 1963).

116. Neville, H. G., "Insurance for Data Processing Users," in *Data Processing Yearbook—1965,* American Data Processing, Detroit, Michigan, 1964, pp. 99–102.

117. Pantages, A., "Problems [Legal and Other] of Packaged Programs," *Datamation, 14,* 75, 76, 79 (April 1968).

118. Poole, A. L., U.S. Patent No. 3,107,343, "Information Retrieval System" [Locates a Desired Record by Means of Control Word Imbedded in the Record or Tape], Filed November 27, 1959; Granted October 15, 1963.

119. Popper, H. R., "Method Claims for Protecting Programmable Processes," in *Proc. 1st*

Law of Software Conf., Washington, D.C., October 1968 (I. Kayton, ed.), George Washington Univ., Washington, D.C., 1968, pp. B-55–B-75.

120. Prosser, F., "Software Copyrights" [Letters re University of Indiana], *Datamation,* **11**, 15 (December 1965).

121. Puckett, A. W., "Limits of Copyright and Patent Protection for Computer Programs," in *ASCAP Copyright Law Symposium,* **1967**, 16.

122. Puckett, A. W., "Protecting Computer Programs," *Datamation,* **73**, 55–60 (November 1967) [CR Rev. 14,396].

123. Rackman, M. I., "Patentability of Computer Programs," *N.Y.U. Law Rev.,* **38**, 981 (1963).

124. Rackman, M. I., "Legal Protection of Computer Programs," *J. Patent Office Soc.,* **48**, 275–277 (April 1966).

125. Rackman, M. I., "Re: Legal Protection of Computer Programs" [Katoona, *J. Patent Office Soc.,* **47**, 955 (December 1965)], *J. Patent Office Soc.,* **48**, 275–277 (April 1966).

126. Ringer, B. A., "Review of Copyright Law Revision," Presented at 1967 American University Copyright Law Revision Symposium, April 20, 1967, pp. 2–5, mimeographed.

127. Rosen, S., "Programming Systems and Languages. A Historical Survey" [Legal Protection of Programs], *AFIPS Conf. Proc.,* **25**, 1 (Spring 1964).

128. Schiffer, G., "Computers and Copyright Law Revision," *Bull. Copyright Soc.,* **11**, 404–408 (August 1964) [CR Rev. 8815].

129. Schimmel, J., "Patent Office Viewpoint Concerning Patentability of Computer Programs," Paper presented at Federal Bar Association Session on Legal Protection of Computer Programming, Washington, D.C., September 1968.

130. Seidel, A. H., "Antitrust Patent and Copyright Law Implications of Computer Technology," *J. Patent Office Soc.,* **44**, 125 (February 1963); *Antitrust Bull.,* **6**, 549 (1961).

131. Siegel, I. H., "Dominance of Sole Patentees in Computer-related Technology," *IDEA,* **8**, 45–50 (Spring 1964).

132. Sizemore, R. C., "U.S. Seeks Patent Ban on EDP Programming," *Electronic News,* **1967**, 30 (March 6).

133. Smith, L. W., "What is Proprietary in Mathematical Programming?," *Comm. ACM,* **4**, 542–594 (December 1961).

134. Sophar, G. J., et al., *Copyright Problems Affecting Communication in Sciences and Education,* Committee to Investigate Copyright Problems, Washington, D.C., December 13, 1961, 25 pp. [PB 177 000].

135. Swenson, J. R., "Software and Copyright" [Letter], *Datamation,* **10**, 10 (December 1964).

136. Titus, J. P., "Copyrighting Computer Programs," *Comm. ACM,* **9**, 879–890 (December 1966).

137. Titus, J. P., "Pros and Cons of Patenting Computer Programs," *Comm. ACM,* **10**, 126–127 (February 1967).

138. von Loesch, T., *Legal Consequences of the Use of Technological Equipment in Public Administration,* Joint Nuclear Research Center, ISPRA (Estab., Sci. Info. Process Ctr.), Italy April 1963, 28 pp (in German) [NASA: N63-17237].

139. Wiessman, C., "Programming Protection: What Do You Want to Pay?," *SDC Magazine,* **10**, 30–31 (July–August 1967).

140. Wessel, M. R., "Legal Protection of Computer Programs," *Harvard Business Rev.,* **43**, 97–106 (March–April 1965) [CR Rev. 8468].

141. Wessler, J., "Change on Software Patents Urged," *Electronic News,* **1967,** (May 8).

142. Wessler, J., "Patentability: No Decision Yet on Software," *Electronic News,* **1968,** 37 (February 19).

143. Wessler, J., "Program Patent Problem Splits Panelists at FJCC," *Electronic News,* **1967,** 36 (November 20).

144. Westin, A. F., "Science, Privacy and Freedom" [Letter], *Comput. Autom.,* **13,** 8 (April 1964).

145. "ACM Committee on Copyrighting Protests Proposed New Bill as Too Restrictive on Use of Computers," *Comm. ACM,* **9,** 461–462 (June 1966).

146. "ADR Receives First Program Patent" [3,380,029], *Datamation,* **14,** 91 (July 1968).

147. "Antitrust Investigation of Software Is Urged," *Computerworld,* **2,** 11 (June 19, 1968).

148. "Basic Patent Challenged: Is Eniac Patent a Fraud? Honeywell Tells Court It Is," *Computerworld,* **2,** 4 (March 27, 1968).

149. "Briefing Conference on Copyright Law Revision" [Information Storage and Retrieval Session], Sponsored by the Federal Bar Association and Bureau of National Affairs, New York, June 1–2, 1967.

150. "Brooks Bill Author Opposes Software Patents," *Datamation,* **12,** 171 (October 1966).

151. "Computer Patent Backed by Court" [of Customs and Patent Appeals: Mobil Oil Software for Analog Computer], *New York Times,* November 23, 1968, pp. 71, 75.

152. *Computer Programs* [Cir. 31 D], Copyright Office, Library of Congress, Washington, D.C., January 1965, 1 p.

153. "Computer Programs Can Be Registered for Copyright," *Publishers' Weekly,* **185,** 102 (June 8, 1964).

154. "Computer Programs Covered in Copyright Law Revision" [Washington Report], *Datamation,* **11,** 21, 133 (November 1965).

155. "Computer Programs: Should They Be Patentable?," *Columbia Law Rev.,* **68,** 241 (February 1968).

156. "Computer Programs to Be Registered for Copyright," *Lib. Congr. Info. Bull.,* **23,** 226 (May 18, 1964); *Modern Uses of Logic in Law,* **1964,** 86 (September).

157. "Copyright Amendment Passes House Committee" [Copyrighted Material as Input to Information Retrieval System], *Datamation,* **12,** 69–70 (December 1966).

158. *Copyright Law as It Relates to National Information Systems and National Programs; A Study by the ad hoc Task Group on Legal Aspects Involved in National Information Systems,* Federal Council for Science and Technology, Washington, D.C., July 1967, 82 pp [PB 175 618].

159. "Copyright Law Revision: Its Impact on Classroom Copying and Information Storage and Retrieval Systems," *Iowa Law Rev.,* **52,** 1141 (June 1967).

160. "Copyrighted Computer Program Agency Formed," *Business Autom. News Rept.,* **5,** 3 (February 8, 1965).

161. "EDUCOM Attacks Pending Copyright Legislation," *Datamation,* **13,** 107 (April 1967).

162. First Law of Software Conference, Washington, D. C., October 22–23, 1968, Sponsored by the Computers-in-Law Institute, National Law Center, George Washington University, Washington, D.C., *Proceedings,* 222 pp.

163. "First Patent Is Issued for Software: Full Implications Are Not Yet Known [M. A. Goetz: Sorting System, U.S. Patent No. 3,380,029], *Computerworld,* **2,** 1 (June 19, 1968).

164. "First Patent on Software, Awarded to Applied Data Research, Reopens Industry-wide Discussion on Problems of Program Protection," *EDP Ind. Rept.*, **3**, 3–5 (July 11, 1968).

165. "First Software Patent. Was Program Patented? Or Was It the 'Technique'?," *Computerworld*, **2**, 4 (July 3, 1968).

166. "F[T]C Member Wants 'Easy' School EDP" [Patent and Copyright Restrictions on Educational Computers] *Electronic News*, **1967**, 33 (April 3).

167. "Guidelines Proposed for Program Patents," *Datamation*, **12**, 98 (September 1966).

168. "Interest Grows in Pursuit of Software Patents and Copyrights," *Datamation*, **12**, 85 (June 1966).

169. "Johnson Unit Says 'No' to EDP Patents," *Business Autom. News Rept.*, **6**, 1 (December 26, 1966).

170. "LBJ Unit Nixes Patents on Programs," *Business Autom.*, **14**, 72 (February 1967).

171. "Legal Information Systems and the Revised Copyright Law," *Valparaiso Univ. Law Rev.*, **1**, 359 (Spring 1967).

172. 1967 American University Copyright Law Revision Symposium, Symposium on Intellectual Property in Automated Systems: Permissions and Payments. Sponsored by U.S. Copyright Office and American University, April 20–22, 1967, Washington, D.C. Selected papers reprinted in *Congr. Rec.*, **114** (June 11–14, 1968), and available from American University in an unabridged edition, 1968, 34 pp.

173. "Ode to Patent Reform Bill Dept." [Computer Programs], *Electronic News*, **1967**, 14 (April 10).

174. "Patent Bill Panics Programmers," *Datamation*, **13**, 93, 97 (June 1967).

175. "Patent Commission Urges Major Changes but Avoids Issue of Government Research," *Wall Street J.*, December 5, 1966, p. 7.

176. "Patent Office Is Ruffled by First Software Patent," *Computerworld*, **2**, 3 (May 26, 1968).

177. "Patent Protection for Computer Programs," *Comput. Bull.*, **8**, ii–iii (March 1965) [CR Rev. 8091].

178. "Patentability of Computer Programs," *N.Y.U. Law Rev.*, **38**, 891 (1963).

179. "President's Commission Says You Can't Patent a Programming Language," *SICPLAN Notices*, **2**, 11–12 (January 1967).

180. *Proceedings of the ACM 20th National Conference, Cleveland, Ohio, August 1965*, ACM, New York, 1965, 563 pp.

181. "Process Patents for Computer Programs," *California Law Rev.*, **56**, 466 (April 1968).

182. "Program Plagiarism Alleged in U.K. Case," *Datamation*, **14**, 91 (June 1968).

183. "Programmers of the World, Arise," *Datamation*, **11**, 103 (February 1965).

184. "Programs for Computers Can Be Patented—Court Rules; Some Makers Oppose Plan," *Wall Street, J.*, November 25, 1968, p. 10.

185. "Proposed Guidelines for the Examination of Applications for Patent on Programming Methods and Apparatus," *Patent Office Gazette*, **829**, 865–867 (August 16, 1966).

186. "Proposed Revision of U.S. Copyright Laws May Have Uncomfortable Effect on Computer Technology," *Comm. ACM*, **9**, 52 (January 1966).

187. "Proprietary Program Progress: 10 Copyrights, One Jail Sentence," *Datamation*, **11**, 19 (October 1965).

188. "Proposed Patent Changes Divide AMA Meeting," *Electronic News*, **1967**, 1, 37 (April 3).

189. "Proposed Patent Changes Exclude Computer Programs," *Datamation*, **13**, 85 (April 1967).

190. "Protection of Computer Programs—Bibliography," *Comm. ACM*, **11**, 67 (January 1968).

191. *Report on the Application of Copyright on Computer Usage*, National Academy of Sciences—National Research Council, Washington, D.C., December 1, 1967, 29 pp [PB 178 367].

192. "Scope of Protection for Computer Programs under the Copyright Act," *De Paul Law Rev.*, **14**, 360 (1965).

193. "Software 'Giveaway' Held Threat [Patent Revision Bill: Morton C. Jacobs Testimony], *Electronic News*, **1967**, 35 (April 10).

194. "Software Patent Raises Questions," *Computerworld*, **2**, 2 (June 19, 1968).

195. "Software, Statutes and Stare Decisis," *Howard Law J.*, **13**, 420 (Spring 1967).

196. "Stock Market Tip; Buy Into Law Firms [Theft of Proprietary Secrets], *Datamation*, **11**, 17 (October 1965).

197. "That Software Patent: Patent Office's Long History Affects Your Rights Today," *Computerworld*, **2**, 4 (July 24, 1968).

198. *'To Promote the Progress of . . . Useful Arts' in an Age of Exploding Technology*, Report of the President's Commission on the Patent System, Govt. Printing Office, Washington, D.C., November 1966, 72 pp.

199. "Where is Software? Copyright Office Asks," *Datamation*, **11**, 111 (April 1965).

200. House of Representatives (87th through 89th U.S. Congress), *Copyright Law Revision, Report of the Register of Copyrights on the General Revision of the U.S. Copyright Law, House Committee on the Judiciary*, Govt. Printing Office, Washington, D.C., Part I (July 1961), 160 pp; Part 2 (February 1963), 419 pp; Part 3 (September 1964), 457 pp; Part 4 (December 1964), 477 pp; Part 5 (September 1965), 350 pp; Part 6 (May 1965); 338 pp.

201. House of Representatives (89th Cong., 1st sess.), *Copyright Law Revision. Hearings on Bills for the General Revision of the Copyright Law, Title 17 of the United States Code, before Subcommittee No. 3, Committee on the Judiciary*, Govt. Printing Office, Washington, D.C., May–September 1965, 2056 pp [Serial No. 8].

202. House of Representatives (89th Cong., 2nd sess.), *Copyright Law Revision. Report of the Committee on the Judiciary to Accompany H.R. 4347. Report No. 2237*, Govt. Printing Office, Washington, D.C., October 12, 1966, 279 pp.

203. House of Representatives (90th Cong., 1st sess.), *Copyright Law Revision. Report of the Committee on the Judiciary to Accompany H.R. 2512. Report No. 83*, Govt. Printing Office, Washington, D.C., March 8, 1967, 254 pp.

204. Senate (90th Cong., 1st sess.), *Copyright Law Revision. Hearings before the Subcommittee on Patents, Trademarks and Copyrights, Committee on the Judiciary, on S. 597*, Govt. Printing Office, Washington, D.C., March–April 1967, 4 parts, 1383 pp, incl. appendices.

205. Ex parte Egan [Patentability of Computer Programs], 129 U.S.P.Q. 23 (Bd. App. 1960).

206. Ex parte King and Barton [Patentability of Computer Programs], 146 U.S.P.Q. 590 (Bd. App. 1964).

REFERENCES

Where the author believes the material in a reference to be basic to the subject area, an asterisk precedes the citation. Such items constitute a short, comprehensive, but by no means complete, set of reference materials.

*1. Nimmer, *Nimmer on Copyright,* Bender, New York, 1969, p vii.

2. Shapiro, Bernstein & Co., Inc. v. H. L. Green Co., 316 F.2d 304 (2d Cir 1963).

3. *Burrow Giles* v. *Sarony, 111* U.S. 53 (1884), p. 58.

*4. Hurt and Schuchman, "Economic Rationale of Copyright," *Amer. Econ. Rev. Supp., Papers and Proc.,* **56,** 426–427 (1966).

*5. McLuhan, *Understudying Media: The Extensions of Man,* Signet, New America Library, New York, 1964, p. 70.

6. McLuhan and Fiore, *The Medium is the Massage,* Bantam, London, 1967, p. 122: "The invention of printing did away with anonymity, fostering ideas of literary fame and the habit of considering intellectual effort as private property. Mechanical multiples of the same text created a public—a reading public. The rising consumer-oriented culture became concerned with labels of authenticity and protection against theft and piracy. The idea of copyright—'the exclusive right to reproduce, publish, and sell the matter and form of a literary or artistic work'—was born."

*7. Muller, "Electronic Computers: Storage and Retrieval," in *Automated Information Systems and Copyright Law, A Symposium* (Hattery and Bush, eds.), American Univ., Washington, D.C., 1968, pp. 12–13. [Unabridged reformated edition taken from 114 *Congressional Record,* June 11–14, 1968.]

*8. However, one eminent authority has a contrary view based upon what *could* be done with certain existing techniques. See Licklider's testimony in *Hearings on H.R. 8809, A National Science Research Data Processing and Information Retrieval System* before U.S., Congress, House, Committee on Education and Labor, 91st Cong., 1st sess., April 29–30, 1969, pp. 240–241.

9. See, e.g., the notice in Samuelson, *Economics: An Introductory Analysis,* McGraw-Hill, New York, 1967, p. vi: "No part of this publication may be reproduced, stored in a retrieval system, or transmitted in any retrieval system, or transmitted in any form or by any means, electronic, mechanical, photocopying, recording, or otherwise, without the prior written permission of McGraw-Hill, Inc."

10. Rosenberg, *The Death of Privacy,* Random House, New York, 1969, p. 97.

11. *Ibid.,* p. 100.

12. Holland, "Futures: A Now-Summary of the EDUCOM Symposium on the Computer and Humanistic Studies," *Computers and the Humanities,* **2,** 57 (1967): "Some scholars use the computer to provide frequency lists of word of other occurrances in bodies of material much too large for mere mortals to manage. Similarly, the computer can scan large amounts of material for accidentals so as to solve attribution problems. It can collate texts with a speed and accuracy far beyond a man's. The making of a concordant—traditional pastime of English vicars—has become common place. John Bartlett took forty years to make his *Concordance to Shakespeare* (producing the *Familiar Quotations* as a kind of by-product); today at Cornell, the job could be done in a month."

13. See the directory of "Literary Materials in Machine-Readable Form," *Computers and the Humanities,* **1,** 75–102 (1967); **2,** 133–144 (1968); **3,** 225–239 (1969).

14. *Language and Machines, Computers in Translation and Linguistics,* National Research Council, Washington, D.C., 1969, p. 19: "'Machine Translation' presumably means going by algorithm from machine-readable source text to useful target text without recourse to human translation or editing. In this context, there has been no machine translation of general scientific text, and none is in immediate prospect." But see Titus, "Nebulous Future of Machine Translation," *Comm. Assoc. Computing Machinery,* 189–191 (March 1967), for some contrary views.

15. Scharfenberg, Smith, and Villani, "A Concordance Generator," *IBM Systems J.,* **3,** 104–111 (1964).

*16. Stevens, *Automatic Indexing: A State of the Art Report* [NBS Monograph 91], National Bureau of Standards, Washington, D.C., 1965, p. 3.

17. Lipton, "Extent of Copyright Protection for Law Books," *Second ASCAP Copyright Law Symposium,* **1946,** 11.

18. *College Entrance Book Co.* v. *Ansco Book Co.,* 119 F.2d 874 (2d Cir. 1941).

19. *Wihtol* v. *Crowe,* 309 F.2d 277 (8th Cir. 1962).

20. Ref. *16,* p. 41.

21. Ref. *1,* §34.

22. *LITE, Legal Information Through Electronics,* hearing before U.S., Congress, House, Subcommittee of the Committee on Government Operations, 90th Cong., 1st sess., August 1, 1967. In addition to the testimony of August 1, the Subcommittee reprinted the LITE Issue of the *AF JAG Law Rev.,* 8(6), 1–51 (November 1966), which gives a eulogistic description of the LITE system. See also U.S., Congress, House, Committee on Government Operations, *Air Force Project LITE,* 90th Cong., 2d sess., February 29, 1968, H. Rept. 1133. Among the questions *not* raised by the subcommittee were: (a) The legality of the Air Force restrictions upon subsequent use by non-Governmental users of the LITE data base tapes: these appear to use the lease method to obtain copyright-like benefits for the government despite the explicit prohibition of Sec. 8 of the Copyright Act, 17 U.S.C. Further, they require the lessee to furnish the government with copies of any results of its research, a practice which would probably be illegal per se under the antitrust laws if followed by a private party, cf. Turner, *Antitrust Enforcement Policy,* 29 A.B.A. Antitrust Section Rep. 187, 188 (1969). (b) The propriety of the University of Pittsburgh, the contractor to the Air Force, in allowing private parties to use the Air Force data base in successful litigation against the Government; see, e.g., "Computer search in amicus brief [*C.I.R.* v. *Brown,* 380 U.S. 563 (1965)]," *M.U.L.L.* [*Jurimetrics J.*], 36–38 (March 1966).

*23. Frankel, "Legal Information Retrieval," in *Advances in Computers,* Vol. 9, Academic, New York, 1969, p. 141: "Also project LITE makes extensive use of KWIC indexes, as a form of output of searches, and as a form of dissemination of information. For example, LITE, published KWIC indexes of the *total text* of Titles 10, 32, 37, 50, and 50 Appendices of the U.S. Code all of which have particular application to the defense establishment, and of *the scope lines of the decisions* of the Comptroller General of the United States. Also complete cross-indexes of the Internal Revenue Code and of other legal texts were constructed [emphasis added and references omitted]."

*24. *Opinion of Attorney General of State of New York,* 142 U.S.P.Q. 288 (1964).

*25. Gorman, "Copyright Protection for the Protection and Representation of Facts," *Harvard Law Rev.,* **76** 1569–1605 (1963), pp. 1603–1604: "In dealing with fact works, courts feel more competent to exercise judgment on matters of creativity and originality; they deal with fewer problems of aesthetics, with standards less subject to change over time. They have thus occasionally fashioned theories of copyright protection which deny the monopoly right to efforts which seem clearly deserving. The map cases come most quickly to mind. In those hybrid cases of fact works which may embody some element of literary or artistic style, such as common snapshots or representational advertisements, courts again may have been too timorous in admitting works to copyright.

"Although the 'originality' test is a shorthand formula for the features of a work that merit copyright, we should not forget that its application is bound up with practical principles of judicial expertise and that its source, the copyright law, is in turn founded upon public and private interests which assume different guises in different cases. With fact works, courts should find 'originality' in the social contribution made by the accurate gathering, verification, and tangible representation of useful information. If the effect of this is to admit to copyright certain classes of works which now go unprotected, the expansion seems a wise one. It will compel courts to resolve the problems of full copyright protection under the rubric of infringement and fair use, rather than of copyrightability. This, in turn, will offer greater flexibility, enabling the courts to label as 'infringement' those works *which interfere unduly with the monopoly of the copyright holder without bringing a commensurate benefit to the public,* and as 'fair use' those works which interfere but slightly with the copyright monopoly while offering much to society [emphasis added]."

26. *Macmillan Co.* v. *King,* 223 Fed. 862 (DC Mass 1914).

27. Ref. *7,* pp. 24–27.

*28. Kaminstein, *Copyright Law Revision Part 6, Supplementary Report of the Register of Copyrights on the General Revision of the U.S. Copyright Law: 1965 Revision Bill,* Govt. Printing Office, Washington, D.C., May 1965, p. 18.

29. Benjamin, "Computers and Copyrights," *Science,* **152,** 183 (April 8, 1966). Mr. Benjamin is chairman of the board of McGraw-Hill Book Co.; see Ref. 9.

30. "OCR: A Case of Minority Rules While the User Buys Blind" *Computer Decision,* **1,** 22 (September 1969): "The crux of the issue is the need, many users believe, for a uniform standard for OCR equipment in this country to protect users from buying equipment that could become obsolete when a standard is chosen.

"The OCR–B font, adopted by the European Computer Manufacturers Association in 1966, is an alphanumeric upper-and-lower-case character set. OCR–A, adopted by the USA Standards Institute in '66 after six years of development, is a numerical and upper-case set. But a lower-case capability could be developed and added to OCR–A, proponents argue.

"After simmering controversy, the Institute's X3 Committee on Computers and Information Processing directed its X3.1 subcommittee on optical character recognition to study the matter. The subcommittee concluded that OCR–B was not ready in its present form for adoption as a standard. The study showed that some characters—such as 5 and S, 2 and Z, 0 and capital O—resemble each other too closely. An OCR machine has trouble distinguishing between such conflict pairs, the report said.

"In an analysis run, 79 characters of the 113-character repertoire—including numeric, upper-case and commonly used punctuation symbols—produced unsatisfactory results, the study showed. Further, it was found that OCR–B could not be read economically in more than a limited number of machine applications."

The point here is not whether OCR (Optical Character Reading) A or B is better, but rather than even such a limited font as OCR–B cannot "be read economically in more than a limited number of machine applications."

31. For a description of the tremendous advances in cpu performance, see Knight, "Changes in Computer Performance," *Datamation,* **12,** 40 (September 1966).

32. E.g., the NASA RECON System.

*33. This section is taken from *The Copyright Law as it Relates to National Information Systems,* Final Report of the Ad Hoc Task Group on Legal Aspects Involved in National Information Systems, COSATI, Washington, D.C. (April 1967), pp. 11–14.

*34. *To Promote the Progress of . . . Useful Arts,* Report of the President's Commission on the Patent System, Washington, D.C. (1966), p. 13.

*35. Banzhaf, "Copyright Protection for Computer Programs," *Columbia Law Rev.,* **64,** 1274–1300 (1964), p. 1276.

*36. *Computer Programs,* Cir. 31D, Copyright Office, Library of Congress, Washington, D.C. (1965).

37. There are other equally unsatisfactory definitions. The Association for Computing Machinery's 1955 attempt: "Program (1) a plan for the solution of a problem; (2) loosely, a synonym for routine; (3) to prepare a program (IRE). The 1964 Honeywell version: "Program*, (1) a plan for solving a problem. (2) Loosely, a routine. (3) To devise a plan for solving a problem. (4) Loosely, to write a routine. See (routine)." And the 1966 American Standards Association choice: "Program. (1) A plan for solving a problem. (2) Loosely, a *routine.* (3) To devise a plan for solving a problem. (4) Loosely, to write a routine. (5) See *Computer Program. Object Program Source Program. Target Program.*"

It is submitted that when the computing profession itself is unable to define its basic verb, one cannot fault less ept entities for trying.

38. Cary, "Copyright Registration and Computer Programs, *Bull. Copyright Soc.,* **11,** 362–368 (August 1964), p. 362.

39. *Baker* v. *Selden,* 101 U.S. 99, 103 (1880).

40. Wessel, "Legal Protection of Computer Programs," *Harvard Business Rev.,* **43,** 97–106 (March–April 1965). However, compare this view with those of Banzhaf in arguing for the advantages of copyright protection over patent protection for computer programs: "By contrast, copyrights are inexpensive, offer immediate protection, are favored by the courts, and *require little showing of creativity. In return, they offer substantial protection and do not require a wide public disclosure* [emphasis added]," *Comm. ACM,* **8,** 220 (April 1965).

41. U.S., Congress, Senate, *Copyright Revision Hearings,* 90th Cong., 1st sess., 1967, pp. 571–572. See also *Comm. ACM,* **10,** 318 (May 1967).

*42. "Computer Programs and Proposed Revisions of the Patent and Copyright Laws," *Harvard Law Rev.,* **81,** 1541–1557 (1968), p. 1550.

43. Ref. *39;* accord, *Mazer* v. *Stein,* 347 U.S. 201, 217 (1954) ("copyright gives no exclusive right to the art disclosed; protection is only given to the expression of the idea—not the idea itself").

44. U.S., *Constitution,* Article I, §8.

45. *U.S.* v. *Paramount Pictures,* 334 U.S. 131, 158 (1948).

46. *Fox Film Corp.* v. *Doyal,* 286 U.S. 123, 127 (1932).

47. 347 U.S. 201, 219 (1954).

48. Ref. *1,* p. 4. See also the discussion in Ref. *42,* p. 1549: "The rationale seems to be that conferring the limited monopoly which a copyright creates will encourage authors to write and publish by removing fear of plagiarism. A demonstration that copyright will provide incentive to produce and to publish programs while effectively protecting them from copying would thus seem to be the constitutional precondition for the extension of copyright to computer programs. But the courts would probably not declare such an extension of copyright to programs to be unconstitutional just because they disagreed with a congressional declaration of economic need. Although the Supreme Court has declared that legislation passed pursuant to the copyright and patent clause must pertain to objects having a claim to discovery or invention in order to be constitutional, it has refrained from reviewing the policy decisions about whether copyright on a particular work or type of original work would 'promote the Progress of Science and useful Arts.' [Footnote]: U.S. Const. art. I, §8; cf. *Cable Vision, Inc.* v. *KUTV, Inc.,* 335 F.2d 348, 353 (9th Cir. 1964), *cert. denied,* 379 U.S. 989 (1965). Arguments have been made that a program is not a work of authorship or a writing in the constitutional sense and thus not subject to copyright. *E.g., Hearings,* pt. 3, p. 776. See also *Mazer* v. *Stein,* 347 U.S. 201, 219–21 (Douglas, J., dissenting). Also, if the statutory language and history were vague, it could be argued that the courts should decide if programs meet copyright's policy test. But since copyright has come to include objects far removed from literary works and since the bill read together with its congressional history does not seem vague, this Note will assume that the copyrightability of programs is not judicially reviewable."

49. 27 U.S. 1 (1829).

50. *Ibid.,* p. 3.

51. *Ibid.,* p. 18.

52. 17 U.S.C. §4.

53. Ref. *35,* pp. 1279 and 1280: "Although no clear-cut definition of the word 'writing' emerges from a study of either the statute or case law, three prerequisities have been suggested by cases and commentators; permanence, tangibility, and a form capable of being copied. These standards are clearly met by programs recorded in any of the principal media

of printing, punched cards and magnetic tapes. However, two additional criteria—visibility and readability—have been suggested by older cases. Upholding the copyrightability of photographic reproductions, the Supreme Court stated in dictum that the idea in the mind of the author must be given *'visible* expression.' In another context, the Court held that a player piano roll was not an infringing copy of copyrighted sheet music because it did not appeal 'to the eye' and was not 'intended to be read,' unlike the ordinary piece of sheet music which to those skilled in the art 'conveys by reading' definite impressions of the melody. Under these additional requirements, while printed programs could be copyrighted, programs on magnetic tape would not be eligible for protection and programs represented by punched cards would fall into some intermediate category. On the other hand, it should be noted that copyrights have been granted to works (such as microfilms) that are too small to be read by the naked eye. Moreover, the effect of the decision in the player piano case may have been weakened by subsequent amendments to the Copyright Act and technological change with the passage of time. In any case, even if sustained by the courts, visibility and readability are statutory rather than constitutional limitations and subject to revision by Congress.

"The indefiniteness of the statutory category 'writings,' a category defined largely by a process of inclusion and exclusion in individual cases, suggests that the copyrightability of a work may be determined less by abstract analysis than by comparison with similar works that have either been granted or denied protection in the past. A printed program is most clearly analogous to copyrighted works composed of numbers and code words— for instance, a code book, freight tariff table, interest and discount table, and a handwriting chart. Programs on punched cards are also analogous to decks of flash cards for which copyright protection is available. Both types of programs are probably copyrightable. On the other hand, magnetic tapes—because they are recordings of information, invisible to the naked eye, that can be reproduced with the aid of a machine—are technically similar to phonograph records for which copyright registration has been refused. This does not, however, preclude copyrights for magnetic tapes. The denial of protection for records is based upon a particular interpretation of the Copyright Act; the statutory provision for a special, limited protection against infringement of musical compositions by mechanical reproductions has been held to indicate a congressional intent not to grant copyrights to such works. Since computer programs are not musical compositions, the statute does not preclude protection for taped programs simply because of technological similarities to phonograph records. In any case, there would be no constitutional difficulties to legislating protection for magnetic tapes.

"Another analogy to taped programs may be found in videotapes, magnetic tape recordings of television pictures and sound. The two are alike in that neither can be perceived without the aid of an electronic device; they differ in that one is basically a recording of a picture and the other of printed characters. The copyrightability of videotapes has not been tested in the courts, although they have recently been accepted for registration by the Copyright Office [footnote omitted]."

54. Ref. *1*, p. 345.
55. *Public Affairs Associates* v. *Rickover*, 268 F. Supp. 444 (D.D.C. 1967). See also Ref. *1*, §95, pp. 357–359.
56. Ref. *1*, p. 359. See also *Annual Report of the Register of Copyrights for the Fiscal Year ending June 30, 1969*, Library of Congress, Washington, D.C., 1969, pp. 12–13: "The growing number of cases that have stressed the weight of the certificate of registration was increased by the holding in *United Merchants and Manufacturers, Inc.* v. *Sarne Co.*, 278 F. Supp. 162 (S.D.N.Y. 1967), that the 'certificate of registration constitutes prima facie evidence of the facts stated therein and, in the absence of contradictory evidence, is sufficient proof to establish a valid copyright.'

"A particularly interesting decision dealing with the evidentiary value of the certificate was *Norton Printing Co.* v. *Augustana Hospital*, 155 U.S.P.Q. 133 (N.D. Ill. 1967), in which Judge Decker, in denying a pretrial motion to dismiss a case involving forms for use in connection with medical laboratory tests, referred to the statement in the *Regulations of the Copyright Office,* 37 C.F.R. §202.1(c), that 'works designed for recording information which do not in themselves convey information' are not copyrightable and cannot be the basis for registration. He concluded that since registration had been made it was 'prima facie evidence that the Copyright Office considered that these forms convey information.'

"The effect of a certificate of registration was also an issue in *Gardenia Flowers, Inc.* v. *Joseph Markovits, Inc.,* 280 F. Supp. 776 (S.D.N.Y. 1968), where the court stated that the certificate initially places the burden 'upon the defendant to produce sufficient evidence to overcome this presumption of validity,' but that proof by defendant of facts contrary to the certificate 'shifts the burden of overcoming such evidence to plaintiff . . . even upon issues over which the Register may have exercised his discretion, for such exercise is subject to judicial review.' "

*57. Nelson, "Copyrightability of Computer Programs," *Arizona Law Rev.,* **7,** 204, 208 (1966).

58. *Annual Report of the Library of Congress 1965,* Govt. Printing Office, Washington, D.C., 1966, p. 84.

59. *Computers and Automation,* **18,** 5 (May 1969), p. 20:

> COMPUTER ART AND MUSIC FESTIVAL—
> CALL FOR CONTRIBUTIONS
>
> The Second Annual ACM Computer Art and Music Festival will be held August 26–28, 1969, in San Francisco in conjunction with the ACM 1969 National Conference. Individuals are invited to submit computer-generated art, music, or sculpture for display at the Festival.

60. Davidow, Foreword to *Music by Computers,* Von Forester and Beauchamp, eds., Wiley, New York, 1969, p. ix. This most interesting book is divided into three broad areas: (1) Programs and systems—crudely put, computer generation of music-like sounds; (2) Algorithms in composition; and (3) Aesthetics.

61. Ref. *58,* p. 85.

*62. See "Study 3, The Meaning of 'Writings' in the Copyright Clause of the Constitution," in *34 Studies for the Committee on the Judiciary,* U.S., Congress, Senate, 86th Cong., 1st and 2nd sess., 1960–1961.

*63. As noted by Kaplan, *An Unhurried View of Copyright,* Columbia Univ. Press, N.Y., 1967, p. 118, from Overhage and Harman, eds., *Intrex: Report of a Planning Conference on Information Transfer Experiments,* M.I.T. Press, Cambridge, Massachusetts, 1965, pp. 34 and 35: "Be that as it may, the members of the on-line intellectual community work in close partnership with the system—with the computer(s) and the information base(s)— in almost all their work, whether it be formulative thinking, or experimentation involving the control of apparatus, or teaching, or learning, or any of the other things in the list of their activities. Many of the members of the community are skilled in the art of computer programming and fluent in a number of programming languages. These people contribute in an important way to the improvement or extension of the system whenever, in the course of their work, they come to points at which the existing facilities are less than satisfactory—and prepare new procedures to fulfill the required functions or to meet the new circumstances. In that way, they add to the processing capabilities of the system. Other members of the community, not given to programming, may nevertheless add materially to the capability of the system; they do so by introducing new facts, new data, and new documents into the store.

"The system is augmented not only through the contributions of its users, of course, but also through the contributions of full-time organizers, programmers, and maintainers of the system. The contributions of the system professionals were greatest during the early years of the development of the system. During the later years, the fact that the substantively oriented users predominate so greatly in sheer number offsets the greater concentration and, on the whole, greater skill of the professionals. *In many instances, however, it is difficult to distinguish clearly between the contributions of the system professionals,* for the professionals monitor the contributions of the users and often modify substantially, and usually polish, the techniques and programs and the sets of data that are offered to the public files [emphasis added]."

64. Kaplan, Ref. *63,* p. 118.

*65. Reichart, ed., *Cybernetic Serendipity: the Computer and the Arts,* Praeger, Washington, D.C., 1969.

66. *Ibid.,* jacket. See also the Introduction, p. 5: *"Cybernetic Serendipity* deals with possibilities rather than achievements, and in this sense it is prematurely optimistic. There are no heroic claims to be made because computers have so far neither revolutionized music, nor art, nor poetry, in the same way that they have revolutionized science.

"There are two main points which make this exhibition and this catalogue unusual in the contexts in which art exhibitions and catalogues are normally seen. The first is that no visitor to the exhibition, unless he reads all the notes relating to all the works, will know whether he is looking at something made by an artist, engineer, mathematician, or architect. Nor is it particularly important to know the background of the makers of the various robots, machines and graphics—it will not alter their impact, although it might make us see them differently.

"The other point is more significant.

"New media, such as plastics, or new systems, such as visual music notation and the parameters of concrete poetry, inevitably alter the shape of art, the characteristics of music, and the content of poetry. New possibilities extend the range of expression of those creative people whom we identify as painters, film makers, composers, and poets. It is very rare, however, that new media and new systems should bring in their wake new people to become involved in creative activity, be it composing music, drawing, constructing or writing.

"This has happened with the advent of computers. The engineers for whom the graphic plotter driven by a computer represented nothing more than a means of solving certain problems visually have occasionally become so interested in the possibilities of this visual output, that they have started to make drawings which bear no practical application, and for which the only real motives are the desire to explore, and the sheer pleasure of seeing a drawing materialize. Thus people who would never have put pencil to paper, or brush to canvas, have started making images, both still and animated, which approximate and often look identical to what we call 'art' and put in public galleries.

"This is the most important single revelation of this exhibit."

67. Ref. *5,* p. 306.

68. Ref. *1,* p. 18.

69. 100 U.S. 82 (1879).

70. Diggins and LeBlanc, *What the Businessman Should Know About: Patents and Trademarks,* Public Affairs Press, Washington, D.C., 1958, p. 2.

71. Ref. *1,* pp. 19–20, citing *Gelles-Widmor Co.* v. *Milton Bradley Co.,* 313 F.2d 143 (7th Cir. 1963).

72. Duggan, review of Ref. *73, Computing Rev.,* **10**(2), 77 (February 1969) [CR Rev. 16,113].

*73. Sophar and Heilprin, *The Determination of Legal Facts and Economic Guideposts with Respect to the Dissemination of Scientific and Educational Information as It Is Affected by Copyright—A Status Report,* Committee to Investigate Copyright Problems Affecting Communication in Science and Education, Washington, D.C., 1967.

*74. U.S., Congress, House Committee on the Judiciary, *Report No. 2237 on H.R. 4347,* 89th Cong., 2nd sess., October 12, 1966.

75. *Ibid.,* p. 58.

76. Ref. *1*, pp. 646–647.
77. Ref. *74*, p. 61.
*78. *Rosemount Enterprises* v. *Random House*, 366 F.2d 303 (2nd Cir. 1966). See also "New Technology and the Law of Copyright: Reprography and Computers," *U.C.L.A. Law Rev.*, **15**, 938 (1968).
79. For a sanguinary view of the threat of present technology to traditional publishing see Gipe, *Nearer to the Dust: Copyright and the Machine*, Williams and Wilkins, Baltimore, 1967; e.g., "Fair Use is a Many-Splintered Thing," pp. 63–81. The publisher, Williams and Wilkins, has a suit pending against the United States charging that it is *not* fair use for the federal government to photocopy medical journal articles for requestors or an individual basis; U.S. Court of Claims, No. 7368 (February 27, 1968). Basic sources for a discussion of fair use include among many others: *(a) Bishop, "Fair Use of Copyrighted Books," *Houston Law Rev.*, **2**, 206 (1964). *(b) Yankwich, "What is Fair Use?," *Univ. Chicago Law Rev.*, **22**, 203 (1954); (c) Lipton, Ref. *17;* *(d) Chaffee, "Reflections on the Law of Copyright," *Columbia Law Rev.*, **45**, 503 (1945).
*80. Baker, *Antitrust Aspects of the Software Issue*, Antitrust Division, U.S. Department of Justice, Washington, D.C. (March 4, 1969). See also *Fortner Enterprises* v. *United States Steel*, 89 S.Ct. 1252 (1969).
81. *Strauss* v. *American Publishers Association*, 231 U.S. 222 (1913).
82. *U.S.* v. *International Business Machines*, Consent Decree (January 25, 1956) CCH 1956 Trade Cases ¶68,245.
83. As cited by Baker, Ref. *80:* "*U.S.* v. *Jerrold Electronics Corp.*, 187 F. Supp. 545 (E.D. Pa. 1960), aff'd per curiam, 365 U.S. 567 (1961) (untried product in infant industry, viz., CATV); *Dehydrating Process Co.* v. *A. O. Smith Corp.*, 292 F.2d 653 (1st Cir. 1961) (extensive record of difficulty when one product used without the other); and *Susser* v. *Carvel Corporation*, 332 F.2d 505 (2nd Cir. 1964), (high cost of setting controlling standards for tied product). Cf. *Baker* v. *Simmons Company*, 307 F.2d 458, 466–469 (1st Cir. 1962) (upholding requirement that promotional sign using trademark only be displayed in conjunction with trademark owner's product.)
84. Ref. *42*, p. 1557.
*85. Rosenfield, *Major Problems of Copyright Law . . .*, National Education Assoc., Washington, D.C., 1968, pp. 17–19: U.S., Congress, Senate, National Commission on New Technological Uses of Copyrighted Works (90th Cong., 1st sess., S. 216, S. Rept. 640, 1967).
86. Kaplan, Ref. *63*, pp. 119–122.
*87. Patterson, *Copyright in Historical Perspective*, Vanderbilt Univ. Press, Nashville, Tennessee, 1968, pp. 19 and 229.
88. Current computer speeds are measured in 5–10 nanoseconds per operation. A nanosecond, roughly put, is the time it takes an electrical impulse moving at the speed of light to travel one foot.
89. Ref. *6*, p. 138.

MICHAEL A. DUGGAN

The Viewpoint of an Author

WRITING—A LABOR OF LOVE?

It was a temptation that this author could not resist—to introduce a viewpoint on copyright in the Encyclopedia which he co-edits. It provided an opportunity to be introspective about one's motives for writing and for entering into contractual obligations with publishers in order to assure distribution of the product—the book, the monograph, the proceedings, the compendium. It also seemed important that the creator of material that is being fought over should be heard from, even with a small voice regarding motivations.

The viewpoint is that of only a single author who has been active over a 15-year period in writing for a specialized field, producing works that have not enjoyed a mass market.

The working environment of this author has been that of the nonprofit institution of higher education in which publication is not stifled, but rather encouraged, or even demanded, if the "publish or perish" concept is to be taken seriously.

It has been said by some that writing is a labor of love—a labor usually so tortuous that some considerable motivations must be present to account for undertaking it not only once but many times.

The labor is at once creative and tedious and exasperating. The creative portion involves the formulation of ideas and the reduction of those ideas to understandable language. The tedious portion involves interminable reading of successive proofs to the point of intolerable boredom. The exasperating portion involves the viewing of the product when first off the press and locating the inevitable misprints that no longer can be corrected.

So what are the motivations that cause an author to subject himself to the rigorous exercise of publication? Some years ago, a European scholar indicated that his institution withheld consideration of his full professorship until his curriculum vitae contained 40 publications. It was a source of amusement to contemplate this mechanistic approach to promotion, until this author examined his own publication record and realized that his full professorship came at that identical point.

At about the same point, invitations to consult and to lecture abroad began to arrive, and it became evident that publication provided a platform for personal visibility that could not be ignored.

And then, of course, the question came up as to why only publishers should benefit financially from one's writings. Why not become a partner in the enterprise of publishing by attempting to share more and more the economic rewards that are the publishers' aims. With this came the realization that the author must think more like a businessman and argue more vigorously for a more substantial portion of the publisher's revenues.

TYPES OF PUBLICATIONS

Books

The writer in a specialized field generally has two media available to him: books and articles.

The book medium can be used as a substantial platform of visibility, since the package carries his own name on the cover, is generally featured separately by the publisher in marketing, and results in secondary announcements and traces of the work through reviews and listings in the catalogs of many libraries and collections. Substantial distribution is assured through the increasing emphasis on "blanket" orders by many libraries.

The book publishing enterpreneur in a specialized field may opt for single or multiple authorship. In the latter case, responsibility is taken by an editor, who decides on content, arranges for authors to write sections or chapters, and reviews the results to ensure attention to the theme of the book.

The trials of single authorship may seem overwhelming to the novice editor, who usually underestimates the effort involved in riding herd over a group of authors who are usually behind schedule and who may be thin-skinned when critical comments are made about their contributions. Those editors who attempt to bypass these difficulties by arranging for symposia which then are to be published as "proceedings" find a decreasing interest in the part of publishers, who find a diminishing market for such works and an abbreviated life for the book, since symposia may often emphasize ephemeral material that could well have been published in journals—or perhaps not at all.

Articles

The medium of journal articles is available to authors who generally find opportunities to publish in professional journals, trade (often "controlled circulation") publications, and "popular" magazines.

The professional journal usually runs the author through the gauntlet of reviewers, who comment critically, usually anonymously, and may cause frustrations for the novice writer. The article is often buried in that it is placed arbitrarily within the covers of a given issue, alongside articles with dissimilar topics, albeit within some specialized field.

The visibility for the author, except in unusual cases, is small, in that the probability of a single article being read by many is diminished. The only traces of the article then are in "contents" alerting publications, and in abstracting and indexing services.

The trade publication may "commission" the writing of an article, and assure greater distribution than the professional journal, particularly when it is a "controlled circulation"* publication. On the other hand, this type of publication is much more ephemeral, with copies often discarded once perused.

Some authors in specialized fields are able to place publications in "popular" magazines, but this occurs so infrequently that it cannot be considered as an effective outlet, particularly for the young author.

---

*This is the type of publication for which there is no subscription fee, with the costs covered through substantial advertising.

COMPENSATION

The author (or editor) who is to be financially compensated for his efforts may find two alternatives offered to him by the publisher: a flat fee or royalties.

The flat fee, more often offered to the contributors to a collective work, is established by the publisher either on a "per page," "per word," or "per article" basis. The fee seems to be established on the basis of the prediction of sales of the work by the publisher. Since it is a fee established prior to the accumulation of any evidence of real sales, it is generally minimal, since the publisher must protect himself against an unexpectedly small market that may not return a profit on his investment.

When royalty arrangements are made, these of course permit the author to share in the risks and rewards of publishing. Very often the royalties are established at a lower rate for some fixed number of copies sold, and rising when the number is exceeded. Sometimes there is a differential rate for sales in the United States and abroad, the latter often being half the former. Sometimes royalties are paid against list price of the publication, other times against gross receipts.

The claim of "standard" royalty arrangements made by some publishers is a fiction, since most such arrangements are negotiable, and *are* negotiated, particularly when the author has a good "track record" from previous publications. Sometimes this negotiation takes the form of advance payments or subsidiary rights.

The argument of the publisher, in attempting to keep royalties low, is that the price for the book rises with royalties and that marketability is closely related to price. The publisher therefore maintains that a lower royalty rate ensures a lower price, a greater market, and therefore greater over-all royalty income to the author. The author is seldom able to evaluate such arguments, not having sufficient experience in the business of publishing, and may shop around with different publishers to try to do the best he can.

Royalties and fees are seldom paid for professional journal articles. Quite to the contrary, for many are asking the authors to pay "page rates" to help cover publication costs and to permit the publisher (often nonprofit) to stay in business.

THE ECONOMICS OF WRITING

The business of writing has been compared by some authors to the job of digging a ditch. It is painstaking, tedious, and fatiguing work. But in specialized fields, the authors usually find that they are fortunate indeed if their hourly pay (whether amortized over total royalties or a flat fee) even approaches that of a ditch digger. More often, the author finds that his efforts may be rewarded by pay that is some small fraction of prevailing minimum wages.

Accordingly, the author must rationalize his investment of time in other terms, in that the visibility attained through publication may lead to promotions, consultantships, and other honorarium-producing activities.

Some, if not most, authors in specialized fields, however, find that the host institutions that provide their regular salaries are sufficiently interested in their writing activities to encourage them through released time, paid sabbaticals, and secretarial support. So the authors can consider their publishing income as "extra" income, and not requiring rationalization on a strict cost-effectiveness basis.

The successful publisher is, of course, fully aware of this situation, and can take it into account in his business negotiations with authors.

AUDIT PRIVILEGES

The new author looks forward with great expectations to the arrival of the first royalty check, and is often disappointed that the world of book buyers has not overwhelmed the publisher with orders. His disappointment is usually articulated in terms of complaints to the publisher that:

—he has not announced the book to enough of the right people
—he has not advertised in enough of the right places
—he has not kept an accurate accounting of the book sales.

The latter complaint may occasionally lead to a request that he be permitted to audit the publisher's business records—after all, if he is indeed a "partner" in the publishing venture, should he not be permitted to share confidential sales information relating to his book?

But trust must prevail, since even if the author could probe the accounting complexities, it could lead to a nightmarish situation where hundreds of authors would be crawling all over the offices annually and preventing the conduct of normal business.

PROTECTION

The protection provided by copyright to an author—usually vested in his publisher—is not often a matter of great concern, until and unless some critical incidents occur.

The ideas wrested from the author's pen are presented to the world in the hope that they will be read, understood, and used. But if the same ideas are discussed by others—without due credit provided to the author—then the question of protection may arise. Copyright then becomes a good thing, even if every or any encroachment, real or imagined, is not prosecuted vigorously by the publisher.

Also, the author of a book which continues to sell over a period of years may become especially sensitive to the appearance of another book which may, or actually does, outdate the book, and threaten the continuing sales. Copyright again becomes important since it does delay the arrival of the competing work, because it forces the next author to expend considerable effort to come up with something new and/or differently organized.

THE DUAL ROLE OF THE AUTHORS

"There's nothing new under the sun" is a good quotation to recall when one is writing. The author must remember that his own efforts depend upon what has been written before. Accordingly, he is, most of the time, a reader of the work of others, and, as he proceeds to collect materials for his book, he often wishes that everything would be in the public domain. How nice it would be to use passages from other writings, of whatever length, that seem to serve his own ends.

Why be bothered by copyright infringment conscience twinges whenever it is convenient to photocopy material? Why is it necessary to contemplate the possibility of royalty payments for photocopying when the material is to be used for the benefit of "society"?

But the mood of the author may change dramatically once his own work is published and the shoe is on the other foot, and others may wish to photocopy his work.

AUTHOR—PUBLISHER RELATIONSHIPS

The relationship between the author and publisher may change with time, depending upon the reputation of the author.

The initial publication contract, when entered into prior to the existence of a manuscript, is binding on both unless the author fails to complete his writing chore, in which case the publisher has no alternative but to withdraw gracefully if not with disappointment. On the other hand, the publisher has cause for concern and even legal action if the book later appears on the list of another publisher.

The publisher generally insists on an escape clause which permits him to refuse to publish if the quality of the manuscript does not meet expectations.

Once delivered and accepted, however, the manuscript proceeds to publication and the copyright action is taken which protects the publisher and presumably the author.

Sometimes the author is permitted, or required, to copyright the book himself, and have the publisher act, in a loose sense, as his agent in publishing the book. In this type of arrangement the financial risk may be that of the publisher alone, the author alone, or shared by both.

POSSIBLE INFLUENCE OF PROPOSED COPYRIGHT LEGISLATION

The attitude of publishers has been that copyright infringements is deleterious to their and the authors' interests, whether the infringement take the form of "fair use" photocopying or other. The publisher whether profit-seeking or not, suggests that the fundamental economic rationale for publishing must be protected. Should this point of view prevail, the mood and resolve of authors may be in for fundamental changes.

If royalties are to be collected for every copying act, and if the publishers are to be protected thereby, then would this not cause a change in the attitude of the author.

The author may well ask: Why should I not be protected as well as sharing in the "residuals"? Why should I not share in the profits of the publisher? If this relationship is indeed a partnership, why not strengthen the partnership by permitting me to be "part of the act"?

The emergence of computer-produced keyword indexes derived from titles of authors' works may pose a question regarding the right of the author to share in the revenues of these new services. Some of these services now demand royalty payments of 1ϕ per "hit" (i.e., a bibliographic citation) that is produced as a result of the processing of computer tapes. An author using these services might have to pay royalty to be alerted to his own publication.

This brief commentary ends here—because the "other shoe must drop" before the story can unfold further. In other words, the attitudes of publishers, both profit seeking and not-for-profit, will likely condition the attitudes of authors and lead to changes in the delicate balances that now govern the relationships between them.

ALLEN KENT

Copyright Revision in the United States

The United States Copyright Act was signed into law in 1909. It has been amended in particulars from time to time, but the fundamental provisions of the act have remained unchanged. It was in many ways an unsatisfactory piece of legislation from the beginning, out of step with copyright as it was developing at the time in the other principal countries of the world, and subordinating the sample protection of authors' rights to a bewildering complexity of technicalities. Enacted when the phonograph record and the silent motion picture were infant inventions, radio and microfilm barely imagined, and television and the computer undreamed of, the statute became progressively more inadequate as the technology of communication went through rapid change. Problems were especially serious in connection with the protection of American works abroad. The 1909 Act had preserved much of the hostility to foreign authors that had dominated American copyright in the nineteenth century, and made it impossible for the United States to become a member of an international copyright convention that would reciprocally provide protection for American works abroad.

Efforts at comprehensive revision of the 1909 Act began following World War I and were primarily aimed at permitting American membership in the Berne Copyright Union, which had become more important with the increasing demand for American works abroad. A serious effort was made in the Dallinger Bill in 1924, and an even more comprehensive effort in the Vestal Bill, which in varying forms remained before Congress from 1926 to 1931, passed the House of Representatives, and failed of Senate passage only because of an irrelevant filibuster. More or less desultory and uniformly unsuccessful efforts were made to revive copyright revision during the 1930s. The most ambitious effort was made by a private, largely scholarly, committee headed by James T. Shotwell and Waldo G. Leland. The bill drafted by this committee in 1939 was introduced in Congress in 1940, but no advance measures had been taken to assure the support of the Copyright Office or of influential members of Congress, and it received no serious attention.

World War II prevented further attention to copyright revision until the late 1940s. At that time the Library of Congress and the Copyright Office decided on the strategy of winning international approval for a new Universal Copyright Convention so designed that the United States could adhere with relatively minor revision of its domestic legislation. It was hoped that the successful negotiation and ratification of such a treaty, accompanied by only such specific revisions of American law as were necessary to conform to the treaty, would make it possible subsequently to undertake a comprehensive general revision without the pressure of acute need for providing international protection.

In its initial stages this plan was successful. Under the auspices of UNESCO, a Universal Copyright Convention was drafted at Geneva in 1952, largely on the basis of proposals presented by the United States delegation, chaired by the Librarian of Congress, Dr. Luther H. Evans. Instead of prescribing a minimum level of protection, as did the Berne Convention, the Universal Convention was based on the concept of "national treatment"—i.e., that each member country would treat works by citizens of other member countries as it did those of its own citizens. The only minimum requirements were that the term of copyright be not less than 25 years, that the right of translation be fully protected for at least 7 years, and that no formality be required for protection of works of other member countries other than a notice in the form of the symbol "©" followed by the date of first publication and the name of the copyright proprietor. The United States could ratify such a treaty without changing its law except to rescind its manufacturing clause as applied to works of citizens of other member countries, modify slightly the notice requirement to permit the new symbol instead of the previously required "Copyright" or "Copr.," and waive the requirement of registration and deposit of works from other member countries except as a prerequisite to suits. These changes were achieved in 1954 and the United States ratification was followed by that of most major countries (except the Soviet Union and China, which entered into no international copyright agreements). Since the Universal Convention contained a provision that it would not be applicable between any two countries both of which belonged to the Berne Union, in practice it served primarily as a treaty between the United States and the rest of the world that recognized international copyright.

With that step out of its way, the Copyright Office turned immediately to the general revision of domestic copyright law, and was given an appropriation to permit a series of exhaustive studies of the issues to be dealt with in the revision. Thirty-four such studies, by highly competent copyright attorneys commissioned for the purpose, were completed between 1956 and 1959, and a thirty-fifth, dealing with the manufacturing clause, was added in 1963. On the basis of these studies, the

Register of Copyrights prepared an extensive report defining the issues and presenting proposals, in some cases alternative proposals, for dealing with them. There were extensive discussions of the report with panels of interested experts, followed in 1964 by the submission of a revision bill drafted by the Copyright Office. This was introduced in Congress primarily to provide a basis for still further discussions, which resulted in a revised bill introduced in Congress in 1965.

Prolonged hearings, involving hundreds of pages of testimony, were held by a subcommittee of the House Committee on the Judiciary under the chairmanship of Congressman Robert Kastenmeier of Wisconsin. These consumed the latter half of 1965, and the subcommittee met with frequency in 1966 to make extensive revisions of the bill. The subcommittee bill was reported to the House of Representatives in October 1966, too late for action by the 89th Congress. It was reintroduced upon the convening of the 90th Congress and reported favorably by the Judiciary Committee in March 1967. It passed the House the following month, with some significant amendments, and went to the Senate. Here again there were extensive hearings before a subcommittee, chaired by Senator John McClellan of Arkansas, of the Committee on the Judiciary, but the committee was unable to report the bill during the 90th Congress. The delay was occasioned primarily by the rise to prominence of two sets of issues which had not had so important a place in the earlier studies of the Copyright Office or of the House Committee. These related to the use of copyrighted works in computers and to the copyright status of works retransmitted by cable television.

It was proposed by the Senate Committee to refer the computer problems to a special commission for study and a report after 3 years, and a separate bill to that effect passed the Senate, but not the House, in the 90th Congress. The problems of cable television, however, were more intractable and complex, with copyright questions inextricably involved with regulatory matters that fall in the province of the Federal Communications Commission and the Congressional Committees on Interstate and Foreign Commerce. These difficulties held the bill in the Senate Subcommittee throughout the remainder of the 90th Congress and the first term of the 91st. In December 1969 the subcommittee completed a revised bill which was printed without awaiting action by the full Judiciary Committee in order to permit the Commerce Committee to give simultaneous attention to those provisions that involved the regulation of cable television. The full Judiciary Committee, however, failed to report the bill during 1970, and legislation died with the adjournment of the 91st Congress. Senator McClellan stated his intention to reintroduce the subcommittee bill at the beginning of the 92nd Congress, so that the whole revision process will remain before Congress. Meanwhile, copyrights that would have expired since September 1962 have been kept in force at least through 1971 by a series of interim extension bills anticipating the generally longer periods of protection afforded by the proposed revision bills.

The principal issues involved in revision are identified below, with brief comments, especially as they relate to libraries or to information science.

TERM

Unpublished works are now protectible under the common law of the several states, which generally speaking provides permanent protection. Published works are protected for 28 years from first publication, and copyright can be renewed for a second such term. This system has been criticized as providing a shorter term of protection for authors than that given any other major country except China and the Soviet Union; as requiring a cumbersome and unnecessary renewal procedure; as impeding the work of librarians, archivists, and scholars through perpetual common-law copyright; as creating confusion because of varying terms of copyright between the United States and other countries in which its films, broadcasts, records, and publications find audiences, and finally, as barring the United States from the benefits of membership in the Berne Union. The revision bill in all its various forms has provided a single term of the life of the author plus 50 years for new works, and an addition of 19 years to the second term of works now under copyright. Joint works would remain under copyright for 50 years after the death of the last surviving author; the term for anonymous and pseudonymous works and works written for hire would be 75 years from first publication or 100 years from creation, whichever is the shorter term. Unpublished manuscripts would remain under copyright for the life of the author and 50 years, but not less than 25 years from the passage of the act and, if meanwhile published, not less than 50 years from the passage of the act.

These provisions would have many advantages, giving authors and their families an assurance as to the life of the estates in copyrights they may leave their heirs, simplifying the administration of copyrights of works broadcast or circulated abroad by providing a term identical with that in the countries with which we have our principal cultural relations, avoiding the complex problem of identifying the date of the first publication of a particular version of a work and verifying its renewal in order to know whether it is still under copyright, doing away with the nuisance and red tape of renewals, clearing up the problem of rights in older unpublished manuscripts, eliminating conforming systems of common law copyright, and opening the way toward a possible adherence to the Berne Union. Though there has been some objection to the lengthening of term, which would be the general though not uniform result of these provisions, they seem generally acceptable and will no doubt be at the core of any revision act finally adopted.

NOTICE

All revision proposals would continue the inclusion of notice as a condition of copyright, but would mitigate the consequences of an unintentional omission of notice, which may now void copyright entirely. Under the revision bill, an author could reinstate his copyright by republishing with notice, but could not recover damages against an innocent infringer who had been misled by the absence of notice in the copies from which it was omitted.

MANUFACTURING CLAUSE

The manufacturing clause of the copyright act now permits only an ad interim copyright of 5 years for a work by an American author not manufactured in the United States, and that only if no more than 1,500 copies are imported. The revision bill would retain the clause, but would raise the import limit to 2,000 copies, permit a full term copyright within that limit, allow the recapture of copyright in a work imported in excess of 2,000 copies by the manufacture of an edition in the United States, and would permit the author to retain dramatic, recording, broadcast, motion picture, photographic, and translation rights in a work not complying with the manufacturing clause. It has also been proposed to exempt works manufactured in Canada from the operation of the clause.

It is generally conceded that there is no logical relation between an author's rights and the place of physical manufacture of a particular form of his work and that the manufacturing clause should not be a part of the copyright act. Printing trade unions and printing and binding companies, however, have been unwilling to surrender this protection, especially in the absence of a tariff on books under the Florence Agreement.

PHOTOREPRODUCTION

There has been an extensive discussion over whether the revision of the Copyright Act should include a specific provision permitting certain photocopying by libraries, and, if so, how the limits of permissible photocopying should be defined. In the Senate and House hearings all interests were agreed that there should not be such specific language, but that the general judicial doctrine of fair use should receive formal recognition in the statute and should continue to govern this issue. Subsequently, however, librarians decided to seek an amendment exempting libraries and their employees from any liability for copies made without profit to the library for a user of the library. The intent was not, apparently, to change the boundary between fair use and infringement but to exempt the library from liability for any infringement on the assumption that the library user receiving the copy would be liable. Nothing in the proposed amendment would in fact, however, have imposed such a liability on the user.

There was vigorous objection to this proposal, and library groups substituted a more restricted proposal that would have given the library the right, even if extending beyond fair use, to make copies of unpublished manuscripts for research or preservation, to make copies for their own collections of damaged or deteriorating works not replaceable from commercial sources, and to make a single copy for a user of a work other than a musical, pictorial, graphic, sculptural, or audiovisual work. Proprietary groups were in general agreement provided the right to exceed fair use in providing copies for users of the library did not extend to works in print or works of which reproductions were available from the proprietor or a licensed source.

The situation was still unresolved in 1970, but the differences had been narrowed. All were agreed on the one hand that "fair use" should be recognized and maintained as a doctrine permitting copying within generally recognizable if not easily defined limits not competitive with or injurious to the author or involving more than incidental exploitation of his creation; all were agreed on the other that multiple copying and the copying of audiovisual, musical, and pictorial works should not be permitted. Librarians were hesitant to rely on the generality and imprecision of the doctrine of "fair use"; authors and publishers feared that a blanket exemption even of single copies that went beyond "fair use" might in a rapidly evolving technology come to be a real threat, especially to scientific and scholarly publishing. But the positions were close enough to make a satisfactory resolution possible. This might take the form of a recognition that the single-copying of excerpts for note-taking or similar purposes is "fair use," that the single-copying of journal articles is "fair use" unless the proprietor makes articles separately available, directly or through licenses to others, either as reprints or as reprographic copies, and that the single-copying of entire works or substantial parts of them would require the permission of the proprietor unless they were out of print and not available in licensed copies. Such a solution would assure that relatively brief excerpt-copying of the usual sort would not suffer interference and that copies of all works would be available to all users from the proprietor or his licensee or a library. At the same time it would protect authors' basic rights and give publishers and microreproduction companies incentives to set up badly needed central services to supply reproductions of journal articles and out-of-print works and protect their investment in doing so.

Meanwhile, all parties had agreed to a reduction from $250 to $100 of the statutory damages for an infringement made by a librarian or educator on the assumption that the copying involved was fair use and to grant the court authority to waive even this reduced figure.

NONPROFIT PERFORMANCE

Under the present law the public performance of a copyrighted work other than a drama does not require the permission of the copyright proprietor unless it is undertaken for profit. This exempts, as it was intended to do, readings and musical performances in schools, churches, and similar situations. But it also has been claimed to exempt broadcast performances over nonprofit radio and television stations, which, of course, were not foreseen at the time the 1909 Act was passed. With the rapid increase in the number and importance of educational television stations, and with the recognition that in other countries nonprofit broadcasting predominates, there was a widespread feeling that authors and composers must be given some rights over the performances of their works over such stations.

This was done in the revision bill by eliminating the exemption for nonprofit performances and substituting a series of specific exemptions that in fact embraced the nonbroadcast nonprofit performances contemplated in the 1909 Act. Broadcasts that are part of an organized program of instruction would also be exempted. The net effect of these changes would be to require the permission of the proprietor for the broadcast of a copyrighted work by an educational station in programs for the general public or otherwise not part of an organized program of instruction.

EPHEMERAL RECORDINGS

Related to educational broadcasting was the right to record a performance and to make copies of the recording, which under the present law would require the permission of the proprietor. Educational broadcasters have sought the right, without obtaining permission, to make ephemeral recordings of such works if the recordings were incidental to performances that would not themselves require permission. Proprietors have been willing to have the law give that right as a part of a revision restricting the exemption of nonprofit performance as indicated above; but have wanted the life and number of copies of such performances limited to those that were ancillary to the original performances. Educational broadcasters have wanted to make an unlimited number of copies to be kept permanently and made available to other stations and users. This issue is unresolved.

COMPUTERS AND COPYRIGHT

The very rapidly growing use of computers and the possibility of their interconnection in communications systems raised many interesting and difficult copyright questions. The questions most actively debated related to the use in computers and networks of existing copyrighted works in traditional formats. Here the problems were what kinds of uses of what sorts of works required the permission of the copyright proprietor, and whether a system of compulsory licenses might be needed when such permission was required but might be unreasonably withheld or not realistically available because of red tape.

Authors and publishers groups sought to protect themselves in the new technology by making the display of a work, as on a cathode-ray tube, a right of the proprietor under certain circumstances; by defining the act of "transmitting" a work to include its communication through a computer network as well as its broadcasting; and by providing that the exemption granted nonprofit transmissions in instructional programs (which had educational broadcasts in mind) should not extend to transmissions initiated by the recipients, as when a student dialed for the next unit of a computer-assisted instructional program.

Some educators, librarians, the federal government, other scientific information specialists, and computer manufacturers sought conversely to have all input of material into a computer exempted from copyright, with control exercised if at all only on printouts that exceeded fair use. Proprietors objected to this concept as unrealistic and impractical.

It was obvious that the issues were complex and rapidly evolving, and could not be immediately resolved. The solution proposed by the Senate Judiciary Subcommittee was to create a National Commission on New Technological Uses of Copyrighted Works which should study the reproduction and use of copyrighted works in computer systems and the creation of new works through the use of such systems and should make recommendations to Congress of needed changes in copyright and procedure. Reprography, except in connection with face-to-face teaching activities, would also fall within its assignment. Meanwhile, the rights of copyright proprietors in relation to computers would remain as they are under the 1909 Act as amended to date. This was a generally acceptable interim solution.

As time passed, the question of the application of copyright to the use in computers of already existing copyrighted works seemed less difficult than had been supposed. Principally this was true because such uses turned out to be very infrequent indeed. And permissions turned out to be much easier to get than had been feared. It became more and more obvious that the truly important copyright questions in relation to the computer would not be those involving the computer's use of works originally created for other purposes. Rather they would be questions of providing a copyright structure that would encourage the fruitful creation and efficient use of materials designed specifically for the computer: e.g., computer programs and systems of materials created for computer-assisted instruction. The design and elaboration of such programs and systems were tedious and expensive, and the investment of time and money required would have to have appropriate protection if it were to come from other than government sources. On the other hand the protection should not be of such a nature as to enable the producer of a pioneering program or system to pre-empt a broad field and prevent its competitive exploitation.

This problem was particularly important in connection with computer programs. In 1970 it was still uncertain whether these could be patented or copyrighted or neither or both. The Register of Copyrights had tentatively accepted the registration of programs for copyright as writings, but the courts had not determined the validity of such registrations. The Patent Office, on the other hand, had been unwilling to grant patents to programs as inventions, but the Patent Court had held that a computer as modified by a program might be a patentable device. Neither form of protection seemed clearly to meet the needs. Patents might require a standard of novelty difficult for a program to meet, and if granted might convey too sweeping a protection. If a copyright protected only the right to copy, however, it failed to meet the problem. The essential right in a program lies in its use, as that in a musical composition lies in its performance. What seemed to be needed was a right easily obtained like a copyright and covering use as well as duplication, but so limited that it could not prevent the use in other programs of the basic algorithms employed in the protected program.

The proposed commission would, of course, deal with this set of problems as well.

CABLE TELEVISION

What had been a relatively minor issue while revision legislation was being drafted in the Copyright Office and considered by the House of Representatives became the dominant one in the Senate. That involved community antenna television, or as it later came to be known, cable television. This technological development began with the erection of tall, specially designed antennae to which many home TV receivers could be connected in order to improve reception in areas where hills, high buildings, or other obstacles impaired the effectiveness of ordinary rooftop antennae. This seemed at first to present no special copyright problems, whether the community antenna was a cooperative neighborhood project or, as more frequently later, a commercial undertaking. But soon antennae were developed that could not merely improve the reception of local stations but bring in distant stations. Moreover, the capacity of a cable system enabled it to offer the subscriber many more channels than could be received over the air, opening the way, and indeed almost requiring, program origination by the cable system.

The copyright issue was essentially whether a cable TV system "performed" a work when it received and retransmitted a broadcast of it and hence whether it required the permission of the copyright proprietor to do so. Copyright proprietors, and especially film producers, feared that if such retransmission, especially from distant stations, were not held to be a performance, a sale of the rights to show a film over TV in say, Philadelphia, could result in its viewing in Harrisburg as well without additional payment, and moreover that it would become impossible to sell exclusive rights in any area, since the exclusivity could be violated by a cable system's bringing in a performance of the work in question from another area. Local broadcasting stations had the same fear: that they would in fact not be able to enjoy an exclusive right for which they had paid.

Conversely, cable systems feared that if they must pay for performance rights they could be "held up" by local stations since they would be compelled to get licenses and would have no bargaining power in negotiations. Similarly, it would be impractical for them to negotiate with the original proprietors to bring in performances from distant stations when those stations themselves did not have permission to transmit a performance of the work to the cable systems area, for the cable system would not know long enough in advance what works were to be broadcast by the distant station and hence what permissions must be obtained. Cable stations felt strongly that as a minimum any requirement that they obtain permission to retransmit copyrighted works must be accompanied by some system of blanket compulsory license. The position of the cable systems was strengthened when the Supreme Court in 1968 in the case of *Fortnightly Corp.* v. *United Artists Television, Inc.* held that at least in the specific circumstances of that case, which involved the unaltered retransmission of a relatively nearby signal, the function of the cable system should be considered as one of reception rather than of performance.

It seemed clear in 1970 that cable television would rapidly move from its role as a sort of amplifier of broadcast signals and become itself a primary originator of its transmissions. This would, in fact, simplify the copyright problem, since no one questioned that a cable system must obtain permission for the performance of works it originated. But it raised enormous and highly controversial questions about the future of a politically very powerful industry in which billions were invested. Copyright became enmeshed in a network of regulatory considerations aimed at determining the relative status of cable transmission and over-the-air broadcasting, the outcome of which could not easily be predicted.

PROBLEMS RELATING TO ACOUSTICAL RECORDS

Phonograph records have always presented difficulties for American copyright law. Four issues have been involved in copyright revision, most of them with a long history of debate. The present copyright law does not recognize a disc, tape, or other acoustical recording as a "writing." Copyright inheres only in the composition as recorded in a written score. But much folk music and much contemporary experimental music is fixed only in a recording and not in a written score. Hence one need has been to permit the copyrighting of a composition which has been given its tangible form only in a recording rather than in a score. This has presented relatively few problems.

More difficult has been the issue of so-called compulsory mechanical rights. Monopoly by the principal recording companies was feared in 1909, and the act of that year attempts to avoid this threat by including a provision for compulsory recording licenses. If a composer elects to allow anyone to make and sell a recording of a performance of his composition, any other record producer may also do so upon paying the composer a royalty, fixed by statute at 2¢ per record "side." Though all supported or acquiesced in the continuation of the compulsory license system, composers and music publishers protested the rigidity of the 2¢ per side rate in the face of inflation and of technological changes that made a side represent 30 minutes rather than 3 minutes. There were also problems of adjusting this rate to other forms of recording, such as tapes, which do not have "sides" in the sense used in the 1909 Act.

A third problem relates to "juke boxes." The 1909 Act, having in mind penny-in-the-slot machines with earphones, apparently without consideration of the potential consequences, provided that performances on coin-operated machines would not be treated as public performances for profit. This has had the effect of exempting the whole very large "juke box" industry from any payment to the composers whose music is performed. Ironically, music played without charge by machine—such as Muzak and similar installations—in a restaurant or night club does require payment of royalties. Composers for years have pressed for a repeal of this exemption. Manufacturers and operators of the machines and the proprietors of the taverns and other facilities in which they are installed have resisted, arguing the difficulty of negotiations with a multiplicity of proprietors and the fear of being held up by unreasonable demands for annual fees if rights were negotiated with a single performing rights society on behalf of all or most composers.

The final problem relates to the rights of performers as distinguished from composers of music. Performers have taken the position that each recorded performance is a distinct work, embodying not only the composer's and arranger's contribution as written down in the score, but also the unique qualities of the rendition and interpretations of the particular performer or group. Hence, they have held that the performers should share in the copyright of the recording as distinct from that of the score. This position has naturally been opposed by film and record companies and music composers and publishers, as well as by what is perhaps a majority of the copyright bar, who feel that though the rights of performers are indeed substantial, they should be protected by contract rather than by copyright law.

The revision bill as developed in the Senate Committee deals with all these issues in a correlated manner. It not only recognizes a phonogram as a means of embodying the musical work for copyright purposes, but recognizes a copyright in the recording of the performance distinct from the copyright in the work performed. Hence, to perform a work by playing a recording of it, save in one of the classes of exempt performances, requires a license both from the copyright proprietor of the work performed and from the proprietor and performers of the particular recording used.

Fixed fees are provided by statute for compulsory recording licenses (0.5¢ per minute per copy for each work, with a minimum of 2.5¢ per copy per work). Compulsory licenses are also provided for the performance of recorded works by broadcast, by background music systems, and by coin-operated machines. For the first two, arrangements are already in existence for compensating the proprietor of the work itself; the statute provides an additional royalty of 2% of net receipts to be divided equally between proprietors of copyright in recordings and performers. For coin-operated machines, an annual fee of $9 for each is prescribed, $8 of which goes to proprietors of copyright in the works performed and $1 to be divided equally again between proprietors of copyright in the records and the performers.

In order to adjust their rates from time to time in the light of changing conditions, and to provide a machinery for determining the distribution of royalties paid under compulsory blanket licenses, the Senate version of the revision bill provides for a Copyright Royalty Tribunal. Panels of this Tribunal may be set up at 5-year intervals on petition of an interested party to review the statutory royalty rates provided in the bill, or annually by the Register of Copyrights if he finds a controversy exists with respects to the distribution of funds received under compulsory blanket licenses. The panels of the tribunal are three-man boards nominated for each case by the American Arbitration Association.

DESIGN COPYRIGHT

A final issue, not originally intended to be dealt with as a part of copyright revision but long under discussion, is the protection of the design of useful objects when not suitable for separate registration as a work of art. The problem has perhaps been most acute in connection with the protection of fabric patterns. A long pending design copyright bill was added as a separate title to the revision bill in the Senate Judiciary Subcommittee. For a 5-year term, renewable for a second 5 years, it would provide protection within certain limitations to new and original designs of useful objects designed to enhance their appearance.

SUMMARY

As this article indicates, though the revision effort has been addressed to the modernizing of the Copyright Act of 1909 in order to deal with the emerging communications technology, the preliminary efforts of the Copyright Office and in large degree of the House Judiciary Subcommittee and of the witnesses who appeared before it were in fact devoted to adjusting the act to the already well-established realities of the 1950s and to remedying already well-recognized weakness. The consideration was primarily of such traditional matters as term, conventional photocopying, recordings, and broadcasts. In general, sound solutions for these problems were proposed and hammered out by negotiation or committee action.

In general the revision effort has *not* come to grips with the genuinely new, or even relatively new, technological developments which will shape the communications world to which copyright will apply during the duration of any new act. Computers, cable television, and new technological developments in reprography and facsimile transmission were not clearly before the minds of the Copyright Office or the House Committee or, in its early hearings, the Senate Committee as major issues in revision. And when the clamor of interested parties forced special attention to these issues in the Senate, it was generally conceded that they had not been sufficiently studied and that indeed society had not yet had sufficient experience with the new technologies to make prudent the immediate drafting of legislation that would govern these matters for unforeseeable decades to come. Hence the proposal of a Commission in Title II of the revision bill to study and propose legislation on copyright in relation to computers and to new reprographic technology, while avoiding present legislative change with regard to computers.

There was resistance to a comparable handling of the cable television issue, on the ground that there were problems crying for present solution. Yet immediate action appeared unlikely in any event, and it seemed highly probable that this issue too might have to be held for future consideration by means of a special commission or similar body.

Hurried action on either computers or cable television seemed unwise, because in both cases the best established and most articulate interests were those concerned primarily with the problems presented by the new technology's use of materials originally copyrighted for other purposes in other formats: the computer's input of material from books and articles, the cable television's retransmission of over-the-air broadcasts. But the real copyright problem—the one of lasting importance—is related not to this parasitism, so to speak, of the new technology, which was likely to be of rapidly declining importance, but to creating a copyright structure that will both stimulate the production of materials specifically for cable television or computer use and facilitate their widespread exploitation. This is a long-range challenge requiring careful thought and much experience with the new media.

Successful copyright revision may well deal promptly with the more traditional issues that are fully understood and for which well thought out solutions exists, while providing by special commission for the further study of the copyright issues presented by the new technology, including cable television as well as computers and reprography.

BIBLIOGRAPHY

Hearings on Copyright Law Revision, Subcommittee No. 3 of the Committee on the Judiciary, House of Representatives, on H.R. 4347, H.R. 5680, H.R. 6831, and H.R. 6835, May–September 1965, Committee print, 1966.

Hearings on Copyright Law Revision, Subcommittee on Patents, Trademarks, and Copyrights, Senate Committee on the Judiciary, pursuant to S. Res. 37 on S. 597, March 15–April 28, 1967, Committee print, 1967.

House Report 2237 on H.R. 4347, October 12, 1966. (Report on the general copyright revision bill by the Committee on the Judiciary, House of Representatives.)

Report of the Register of Copyrights on the General Revision of the U.S. Copyright Law, July 1961 Committee print, House of Representatives.

Studies on Copyright, Arthur Fisher Memorial Edition, compiled and edited under the supervision of The Copyright Society of the U.S.A., 2 vols., Fred B. Rothman Co., 1963. Contains the studies commissioned by the Copyright Office as a basis for revision.

Supplementary Report of the Register of Copyrights on the General Revision of the U.S. Copyright Law: 1965 Revision Bill, May 1965, Committee print, House of Representatives.

DAN LACY

INDEX